BEYOND THE LOCKED DOORS

WOMEN'S SAFETY AT HOME

GUNJIKA V MISRA

G. Premila Raj
National Award-winning Educationist

Clever Fox® PUBLISHING

Chennai • Bangalore

CLEVER FOX PUBLISHING
Chennai, India

Published by CLEVER FOX PUBLISHING 2026

ISBN: 978-93-7500-988-7

DEDICATION

This book is dedicated to my Ma, Mrs. Indira Misra (Late), who loved me like no one else.

I Love You, Ma.

CONTENTS

ACKNOWLEDGEMENTS

I offer my heartfelt *Pranaams* to **Ma Adi Parashakti**, for blessing me with everything I have ever desired in this lifetime. After my biological mother moved on, she became my pillar of support and guided me during moments of doubt. She fills me with fearlessness and helps me choose the right step, at the right time, in every moment of my life. This book would never have been possible without Her grace, and I place this work at her feet with deep reverence and thanks.

I am super grateful to my loving family, who have always been my source of inspiration and motivation. To Late **Mrs. Indira Misra** (Mom) & **Mr. Vishwanath Misra** (Dad), who instilled a love of learning and encouraged me to pursue my dreams. To **Mrs. Manju Sharma**, (Mother-in-law) and **Roshan Ravi** (Brother-in-Law), for being the silent pillars of support & strength in my life. To **Robin**, my spouse, who provided unwavering support and encouragement through the long hours of writing and research. And to my fantastic daughter **Rishika**, who pushes me to become a better mother and a powerful role model for her every day.

I am also grateful to all my masters who have guided me to constantly upskill and uplift myself in every area of life. I would like to thank **Coach Manju K Manohar**(Top 100 Coaching Leaders of India - 2025) who encouraged me throughout the writing process. Not just that she diligently followed up with me over the last two years and ensured that I submitted the book to the publisher Cleverfox publishing Ltd. I will be truly remiss in my duty if I don't mention the name of some very powerful women leaders who have helped shaped my life to the point where it is today: **Dr. Tejashri Kamble** & **Ms. Vinita Verma** (NACO), **Dr. Ananya Chakraborty** (TISS), **Dr. Govind Kelkar** & **Ms. Manjari Jaruhar (IPS)** (Landesa - RDI), **Ms. Shelley Dhar** (Piramal Foundation), **Ms. Viji Arora, Ms. Anubhuti Patra, Ms. Somi Srivastava, Ms. Mary Thanikal (Keerthana), Ms. Roopali Darsha** (Catholic Relief Services), **Ms. Nandita Bhatla, Ms. Nidhi Lamba** (WorldBeing India Foundation) and **Ms. Koushiki Banerjee** (UNICEF).

I would also like to dedicate this book to the women who have shared their stories with me and inspired me to write on this important topic. To the survivors of violence, whose strength and resilience have left an indelible mark on my heart. To the advocates and activists who work tirelessly to make the world safer for women. And to all the women who have faced challenges and adversity but continue to persevere and thrive.

Finally, I dedicate this book to my readers, who have taken out time from their precious schedules to engage with my ideas and reflect on the issues discussed in this book. Your interest and support mean the world to me, and I hope this book inspires you to take action and make a positive difference.

FOREWORD

Smt. G. Premila Raj

National Award Winning Educationist
(from the President of India)
Recipient of the Fulbright Nehru Fellowship (USIEF)
Marathoner

"Women are born free but found in chains…" which is a very famous adaptation of a quote by Jean-Jacques Rousseau.

In the unfolding narrative of life—where dignity, courage, and resilience define our deepest battles—women's safety within the very walls meant to protect them becomes a profound concern. Beyond Locked Doors: Women's Safety at Home shines a clear and unwavering light on this reality.

Caught in the web of life, often woven with endless household duties, sacrifices, and unspoken expectations, many women slowly lose their identity, piece by piece. Their struggles are quiet, their suffering hidden, their dreams pushed behind closed doors. Sometimes, the pain is a tingling ache—subtle yet sharp—and no matter how hard they try, they can't wriggle out of it.

I was introduced to the author Gunjika by my friend and book publishing coach Manju K Manohar. The authors' words resonated with me because she has strived to bring forward the voices, fears, and silent stories of women whose lives have been shaped by domestic violence and societal conditioning. Through thoughtfully presented story-based examples, the author offers a deeper understanding of the emotional and physical challenges faced by women living in unsafe homes.

With the precision of careful research and the compassion of someone committed to meaningful change, the book highlights essential legal protections, government schemes, and little-known resources that can empower women to rise above injustice. It encourages every woman to reclaim her strength, to speak, and to step beyond fear with clarity and determination.

This work not only educates but also inspires—serving as a guide, a companion, and a harbinger of hope. It contributes meaningfully to the ongoing effort to ensure safety, dignity, and justice for every woman.

The book serves as a clarion call—Don't just rely on what the government can do for you.

Change your attitude.

Change your behaviour.

Change your response.

The change should begin from inside.

Beyond the doors, every woman deserves to live not just a safe life but also a meaningful one.

Every woman deserves to have the freedom to open the door and step out and attain pinnacles of success.

ABOUT THE AUTHOR

Gunjika is a daughter, mother, sister, and woman with nearly three decades of experience in the trials that society presents in front of us women every day. She has dedicated her career to helping women stay safe and upskilled daily.

Gunjika is a Biotechnologist, Public Health Specialist and a Data Scientist. In addition to her regular work, Gunjika is the National President – Home & Security at the Women's Indian Chamber of Commerce & Industry (WICCI). In her 18 years of work experience in the areas of Public Health, Land Rights and Child Protection, she has closely worked towards generating awareness and promoting self-reliance among women and girls from all sections of society. She is committed to empowering women. She passionately works to enable women to take control of their safety, both inside and outside their homes. She is passionate about making the world safer for all women.

Gunjika's passion for women's security began when she began working with marginalised women and girls at the National AIDS Control Organization, Government of India. After witnessing firsthand the impact of violence against women in her community and the communities she worked with, she knew she wanted to make a difference.

Since then, Gunjika has worked with Indian and international organisations to develop and implement programs that address women's security issues. She has interacted with millions of women and girls, heard them out, and helped them in everyway possible.

Gunjika is a Research, Monitoring and Evaluation and Learning(RM&EL) expert with around 18 years of experience in national and international NGOs. She is also the founder of 'Handwriting Universe' – a Graphology and Graphotherapy service provider company. With this book, she also wears the hat of a published author. When she's not working, she enjoys pampering her family and spending time with them.

When she is not busy with her professional, personal or social work related pursuits, she would be found relaxing curled up on her couch reading a book or playing with her daughter. At times she likes to dabble in cooking with the help of her esteemed

Guru "YouTube"! She persuades her hubby, mother-in-law and daughter to taste the outputs from her cooking experiments and has so far received 5-star rating from them.

CONTENT WARNING & DISCLAIMER

CONTENT WARNING:

This book contains descriptions of physical and mental abuse, as well as violent acts. Readers who may find such material triggering are advised to skip the passages in italics.

This book is strongly recommended for readers aged 18 and above.

DISCLAIMER:

This book is intended for informational and educational purposes only. It is not a substitute for professional legal, medical, psychological, or therapeutic advice. The experiences, opinions, and strategies shared in this book are based on the author's research and personal insights and may not be applicable to every situation.

No portion of this publication may be construed as portraying actual events or persons, nor should any character or situation herein be interpreted as a factual representation. Any resemblance to real persons or incidents is purely coincidental.

If you or someone you know is experiencing domestic abuse, please seek immediate help from qualified professionals, local support services, or emergency authorities. Always prioritize your safety and well-being.

The author and publisher disclaim any liability, responsibility, or legal obligation for any loss or damage—direct or indirect—that may arise from the interpretation, application, or misuse of the material contained in this book.

This book is intended for informational and educational purposes only. It is not a substitute for professional legal, medical, psychological, or therapeutic advice. The experiences, opinions, and strategies shared in this book are based on the author's research and personal insights and may not be applicable to every situation.

No portion of this publication may be construed as portraying actual events or persons, nor should any character or situation herein be interpreted as a factual representation. Any resemblance to real persons or incidents is purely coincidental.

If you or someone you know is experiencing domestic abuse, please seek immediate help from qualified professionals, local support services, or emergency authorities. Always prioritize your safety and well-being.

The author and publisher disclaim any liability, responsibility, or legal obligation for any loss or damage—direct or indirect—that may arise from the interpretation, application, or misuse of the material contained in this book.

CHAPTER 1

THE BEGINNING OF IT ALL

Scan QR Code to watch: No Means No | Amitabh Bachchan Famous Dialogue

Time: After midnight

Place: A house in India with multiple families staying under the same roof (a common story around two decades in many parts of India)

(Trigger alert: child abuse)

I was a 14-year-old slender girl who had this habit of sleeping on the same bed as that of her mother (which is a common practice in many Asian households where children and teenagers often sleep with their parents on the same bed). I was in a state of deep sleep when suddenly I woke up. My heart was beating heavily. I felt my frocks' hem getting lifted by rough and calloused fingers. I felt frozen with fear, as these fingers were being inserted inside my panties...

Then I felt a deep rush of pain searing through me. This pain was not entirely physical... it was also mental...

The vicious calloused hands belonged to a man from my own family! A relative.

Have you ever felt betrayed by someone close to you? How unfair was it?

I had ENOUGH…

In the darkness, I delivered a resounding kick to the groin area of that man….I heard a pitiful whimper… he could not even scream as my mom was sleeping next to me.

This one kick changed my life forever. This was not the first time that this man had dared to touch me in inappropriate parts of my body.

But this was the first ever time that I was able to summon enough courage to deliver that powerful kick!

It was the first and last time that I had to kick him! That one kick stopped him from abusing me further!

This abuse had been going on stealthily for months before that fateful night. Whenever his rough hands abused me, I used to feel violated like hell. I could not complain to the police(cops) or to the teachers or even to my own parents, because this man was related to my father. This man had threatened to harm my parents, if I were to go public with his name.

At that moment when I kicked him, I must confess to you my dear readers, that I hated every bit of his existence. However, today, nearly 25 years later, I feel grateful to him for allowing me to discover how indomitably courageous I was. He helped me, in his own twisted manner, discover a new side of me - the powerful version of me.

Don't mistake that I justify or condone his wrong-doing! I am just forgiving him for what he has done because I need to forgive him to move on with my life!

That kick changed my life forever, giving me a feeling of great control over my own body. I knew that I could care for myself and did not need anyone else's support to defend myself. The kick that I administered that night gave me an incredible boost of self-esteem that has stayed with me even after 25 years! I have taken 100% responsibility for my security ever since that nightmarish night.

It is commonly perceived that a woman is at her safest at home. However, the situation is often the opposite. Be it gender-based violence or Femicide[1] (the murder of women), subjugation and repression by intimate partners and relatives go a long way in making the home a highly insecure place for women.

All abuses may not even be painful. In some cases, it may be difficult to prove that an abuse has happened. For example, if a doctor while examining the body touches certain body parts for a slightly longer time or if a masseuse or physiotherapist touches certain body parts, we may not be able to prove that an abuse has happened unless we have witnesses or video recordings. Also in some instances, a relative of a child could abuse him or her without causing body pain.

---

[1] Femicide: The killing of a woman or girl because of her gender, often linked to domestic violence and gender inequality.

(Trigger alert: child abuse)

For example, let's take the case of Shalini(name changed to protect her identity). Her cousin who lived with them used to fondle her chest area when she was a 7-8 year old child under the guise of tickling her. This used to happen in front of the elders. They did not see anything wrong with this action until one day an aunt came to visit them. The aunt pointed out that the boy indulging in this act had signs of being sexually excited. After that, the parents started becoming more vigilant and finally warned the boy not to touch the young girl. Both children and their parents need to be taught that any area between the neck and the knees should not be touched by anyone other than parents or a medical professional (under the watchful eyes of the parents). Remember, the person who commits abuse could be doing it in front of you without you being aware! It is not just the female child that might become a victim of abuse. These days, parents of boy children must also be highly vigilant.

The home is the sacred haven of any individual. Insecurity at home for women triggers a vicious cycle of insecurity in their community - the insecurity at home is mirrored in their immediate surroundings, offices, and public interactions.

The social structure existing in the world today is essentially anti-women.

- ⃠ While growing up as a teen and a college-goer in Delhi, I had to assert my security in the form of stomping, kicks, and rebukes towards innumerable abusive men who could not keep their hands to themselves and their tongues under control in public transport, on the road, and in closed spaces.

⃠ At around 28, I fell in love with an abusive and toxic male. I dropped him like a hot potato five years later. I had plans to marry him, but "the kick" saved me by waking me up to that person's reality.

✓ After this toxic relationship, I worked on myself through meditation and attracted my soulmate. My husband is super respectful and loves me to bits.

Violence against women at home is being propagated globally in the following ways (as per reports from the United Nations (UNWOMEN[2]):

- Almost **one in three women (840 million women)** worldwide has experienced **physical and/or sexual violence by close male relatives or experienced non-partner sexual or physical violence at least once**.
- **More than 86% of all physical and/or sexual violence against women** is perpetrated by **current or former husbands or intimate partners such as boyfriends and live-in partners**.
- **Almost one in six adolescent girls in a relationship between 15–19 years of age (17%) has been exposed to physical and/ or sexual violence by an intimate partner or husband.**
- **Less than 40% of women worldwide who have experienced violence seek help. Less than 10% of women seeking help have approached the police.**
- **Fifteen million adolescent girls worldwide**, between 15–19 years of age, **have experienced forced sex.**

[2] UNWOMEN: The United Nations Entity for Gender Equality and the Empowerment of Women, established in 2010 to promote women's rights, gender equality, and women's empowerment worldwide.

- According to the latest UNODC[3] - *UN Women report on Femicide (the murder of women)* ***worldwide, more than five women or girls are killed every hour by someone in their own family.*** **In 2024, around 60% of all murder of women (femicide) were committed by intimate partners or other family members.**

THE NEED FOR THIS BOOK

Scan QR Code to watch: No Means No | Amitabh Bachchan Famous Dialogue

My life experiences until now have taught me that every woman on this planet, irrespective of her age, nationality, caste, creed, and socioeconomic status, faces essentially the same set of challenges and repressions that I had faced.

One way of ending any form of repression is by calling it out and standing up against it.

There is a famous dialogue by one of the leading actors of India, Amitabh Bachchan (in the movie of Bollywood film 'Pink') which is very apt in this context:

[3] UNODC: The United Nations Office on Drugs and Crime, a UN agency that works to combat illegal drugs, organized crime, corruption, and terrorism, and to promote justice and the rule of law worldwide.

"'Na' sirf shabd nahi hai… apne aap mein pura vaakya hai. Isey kisi tark, spashtikaran, explanation ya vyakhya ki jarurat nahi hoti… Na ka matlab na hi hota hai… And when someone says so, you STOP."

(*'No' is not merely a word… It is an entire statement. It does not need any logic, explanation or definition. No means No. And when someone says so, you stop.*)

- Amitabh Bachchan in the Bollywood film Pink (2016)

This one dialogue is so incredibly empowering. It simply reaffirms a long-known fact - just by saying "No" and safeguarding yourself, many mishaps can be averted.

However, the right to say "No" is also closely linked to a woman's agency[4] (the ability to make choices or identify goals and act upon them) in her mind and her household. Examples of the agency are right over her own body, the right to make financial decisions by herself and the right to go out of her house by herself. So many women and girls today have wilfully handed over their agencies to others in their lives - their parents, spouse and in-laws.

Imagine my life without that action I took that night. Imagine the long-term harm of enduring such physical and sexual abuse. My agency, or in simple terms my sense of identity, would have died slowly at my own hands had I not acted that night. I would have been so depressed that I could never even have imagined the wonderful life that I now lead. My non-existent

[4] Agency: The ability to make your own choices

agency would have ensured that I would never even dream of going public with my story of abuse. Forget even writing a book on this topic.

Throughout this book, I want to share experiences that helped me grow and overcome challenges at every stage. You may have heard about all these strategies in scattered nooks and corners of the internet or in some long forgotten reports or books or even in newsreports. In this book, I have taken a lot of pain to collate all this information from various sources and present them all together in an easily digestible format.

As women, we are naturally blessed with a sixth sense of in-depth awareness. We can feel and experience our surroundings profoundly and richly. Keeping this in mind, I have infused visual, auditory and kinesthetic[5] elements in this book.

At the beginning of each chapter, you will see a QR code taking you to a song/video (available for free on YouTube) that I want you to hear and remember as you read that chapter. I will share incidents from my life (successes and failures) and help you through methods like kinesthesia. This book is not a feminist tome[6]. Men are equal victims of patriarchy. In recent years, they have shown great resolve and intent to come out of the shackles of patriarchy and embrace their authentic, empathetic selves. My dad and husband are great examples of this shift.

---

[5] Kinesthetic: Relating to learning or understanding through physical movement, hands-on activities, and bodily experience rather than through listening or reading alone.

[6] Tome: A large, heavy, or scholarly book, often one that contains detailed or serious content.

I sincerely hope that every woman or girl reading this book can assimilate at least one idea from this book. Suppose this book helps even one woman, or girl in asserting her power with innate confidence, I will consider that my purpose has been served.

CHAPTER 2

NATURE'S GIFT: EXPLORING HOW WOMEN ARE BIOLOGICALLY WIRED FOR SUCCESS

Secrets of the X Chromosome

<u>Rita's story of her birth:</u>

Rita overcame a complicated pregnancy to be born healthy and strong. When her mother discovered she was pregnant, there were concerns about her and the baby's health. Her mother had a history of high blood pressure and gestational diabetes, which made the pregnancy high-risk.

Throughout the pregnancy, Rita's mother was closely monitored by her doctors, who recommended bed rest and frequent check-ups. Despite their best efforts, however, complications arose. At six months pregnant, Rita's mother was hospitalised due to Preeclampsia, a potentially life-threatening condition characterised by high blood pressure and organ damage.

Rita's mother remained in the hospital under close supervision for the next several weeks, receiving medication to control her blood pressure and prevent further complications. Despite the risks, she was determined to carry the baby to term. Her doctors worked tirelessly to ensure she and the baby remained healthy.

Finally, after a long and challenging labour, Rita was born. Though she was small and delicate, weighing just 4 pounds, she was healthy and robust. Her mother was overjoyed to hold her in her arms, grateful for the miracle of her birth.......... (TO BE CONTINUED)

Nature and society can often be found standing at opposite ends. This is the same as the standing of women in the human community. It has been believed that women are the "weaker sex". On the other hand, nature considers the female gender as the "stronger one".

From numerous research studies proving that female foetuses are more robust and have better odds of surviving pregnancy than male ones to the more significant number of older women than older men in any community, nature, in infinite ways, has blessed the female gender with greater resilience and a more substantial opportunity to bounce back from adversity than the male gender.

DID YOU KNOW?

The 8,000-year-old Indus Valley Civilisation is one of the oldest human civilisations known to Man. It is also historically known as the Harappan Civilization. Scientists tell us it is even older than the Mesopotamian and Egyptian civilisations. Based on archaeological findings, the Indus Valley Civilisation has been dated between 2600 BC–1900 BC. Its most striking feature was the extent of its urbanisation during a time when technological tools and know-how were non-existent.

Social Scientists believe this highly developed civilisation to be a matriarchal one, i.e., one in which women headed the social structure. This contrasts with the patriarchal (one in which men lead the society) structure prevalent today. This matriarchal viewpoint is based on the popularity of the Mother Goddess in the Harappan Society, as indicated by the finding of many terracotta female figurines in the Punjab and Sind region. Among the most famous images of the Harappan society is that of the Bronze Dancing Girl idol adorning New Delhi's National Museum.

When a woman died in the Harappan society, she was invariably offered wares like dish-on-stand, bowl-stand, beakers and medium-sized vases, denoting her status over and above her male counterparts.

The towns, streets, structures, brick sizes and drains layouts were strikingly uniform, elaborate and well laid out. Historians are still awe-struck by the intricate detailing of the Harappan Social Structure. For the record, the Harappan script is yet to be deciphered.

Nature's Preference: The Surprising Science Behind Why Female Foetuses Thrive.

I am the third surviving child of my parents. My mother had miscarried a male foetus before conceiving me. After the miscarriage, my parents were told that had the foetus been a female, it would have had better odds of surviving the conditions that led to the miscarriage.

My mother's pregnancy with me was the most complicated since she was hospitalised for one whole year during the pregnancy and even after it. This was because my mother had developed a condition called Preeclampsia.

Preeclampsia refers to a pregnancy complication characterised by high blood pressure, high protein levels in the urine that indicate kidney damage, or other signs of organ damage. If left untreated, this pregnancy complication can lead to severe — even fatal — complications for both the mother and baby.

In the 1980s, the treatment involved saving whom the family chose to keep - the mother or the unborn baby. My mom was a wife and already had two very young children, and understandably my family decided to save her.

Consequently, the Unborn Me was left entirely to the mercy of God, as the doctors began focusing more on my mother's well-being than mine. The doctors expected me to be spontaneously aborted due to certain medications they gave my mother. However, I survived.

On 11th July 1982, my mother and I set a record in the hospital where I was born. We were the first mother-baby pair that had survived Preeclampsia. My proud dad went from house to house distributing sweets on this happy occasion.

Being a girl, I survived an adverse pregnancy in which the odds were entirely against me. However, my elder brother could not survive an adverse pregnancy.

The story of the strength of the female foetus continued with my daughter Rishika. I was the outcome of a complicated pregnancy, and so scientifically, my chances of having a problematic pregnancy were very high. Four days after I learned of my pregnancy (when my daughter was five weeks old), I suffered massive bleeding. My gynaecologist was very concerned and told me that no foetus could have survived heavy bleeding like that. She asked me to get a fetal heartbeat check done to confirm the spontaneous abortion and remove the fetal remains from my uterus.

Wholly dejected and heartbroken, I went for the fetal examination. The moment the ultrasound probe was placed at my lower abdomen, a rapid set of "*lub-dub, lub-dub, lub-dub, lub-dub*" (heartbeats; *fetal heart rate is pretty fast*!) blew my mind off. **My baby survived!** I had always wanted a daughter as my first child. Although it was too early to predict the gender of my baby at that time (five weeks), I knew I would have a daughter.

One and half months later, towards the end of the first three months of my pregnancy (first trimester), I spontaneously bled again. This time the bleeding was so heavy that I experienced massive dizziness. My concerned husband instantly took me to the hospital, and I was immediately admitted. I was admitted late at night, so an ultrasound facility was unavailable. The amount of blood loss had shaken me up. I was super scared for my daughter. My husband and I will never forget that one night till the end of our lives… we were so frightened. Chances of spontaneous abortions are always high in the first trimester. The following day, the fetal ultrasound was done.

My daughter repeated the miracle. She had survived the ordeal once again.

My mom's pregnancy with me and my daughter's birth prove one fact that science agrees with. Compared to male foetuses, **female foetuses have better chances of survival not just in the womb, but also during childbirth and after delivery.**

Numerous scientific studies have stated that the male foetus is more fragile than the female foetus (*Vatten and Skjærven, 2004*). Female foetuses have been found to have **greater adaptive flexibility early on in pregnancy** (*Sandman et al., 2013*). Female foetuses have an **advantage over males, with better chances of survival during the perinatal period** (the period between identification of pregnancy to a year after giving birth), **particularly after preterm** (babies born alive before the completion of the standard pregnancy duration of 37 weeks) **birth** (*Brothwood et al., 1986; Cooperstock and Campbell, 1996; Hoffman and Bennett, 1990; Stevenson, 2000; Sheiner et al., 2004; Di Renzo et al., 2007; DiPietro and Voegtline, 2017*).

Studies have also shown that the male foetus cannot adapt to air pollution, and exposure of the mother to PM 2.5 particulate matter can also lead to miscarriage of the male foetus (*Jedrychowski et al., 2009*).

Male foetuses are more sensitive to being negatively impacted due to maternal smoking than female foetuses (*Wertelecki et al.,*

1987; Zaren et al., 2000; O'Shaughnessy et al., 2011). This is particularly important considering the World Bank data on the prevalence[7] of current tobacco use among females (% of female adults) in 2020. While 9 out of every 100 women worldwide were found to be current smokers, **13 out of 100 (~44% more than the world prevalence) Indian women were found to be current smokers.**

The placenta is a specialised organ that forms only during pregnancy. Its function is to connect the developing foetus to the wall of the mother's uterus. It allows for the exchange of nutrients, oxygen, and waste between the mother and the foetus and produces hormones that help support the pregnancy. Any problem in the placenta's functioning leads to pregnancy risk. A study conducted in the year 2000 (*Andrew et al.*) found that severe problems in the placenta are much more common in a pregnancy involving a male foetus than a female one. It concludes by saying that such issues in the placenta coincide with an increased loss of male foetuses in the placenta. All these studies hint towards one fact – *Nature has blessed the female gender with greater resilience to withstand hostile situations right from conception.*

Please answer this question considering all the facts I presented in this chapter.

ARE WOMEN THE "WEAKER GENDER"?

[7] Prevalence is a proportion of individuals in a population who have a particular disease or condition at a specific time. Essentially, it describes how common a particular health issue is in each population. For example, if 10 out of 100 people in a community are smokers, the prevalence of diabetes in that community is 10%.

Based on the scientific evidence and research, our answer would be a resounding NO.

Miracle of Life: The Incredible Power of Women to Create and Nurture

Of the two genders walking this planet, only the female gender has been given the power of conceiving, maintaining and giving birth to an entirely new Human Being.

Smile if you agree that most of us take this power for granted. Historically and today, society does not give this gift the respect it deserves. It is perceived that a woman is BOUND to give birth

In Hindu mythology, the Divine Feminine is worshipped for her power of Creation. However, the same logic does not hold for human females who do the same thing — creation. Another miracle related to this ability to give birth in females is the ability of the mother to provide complete nutrition for the newborn baby in the form of breast milk. For the first six months of life, a baby is allowed nothing, not even water, apart from its mother's breastmilk.

Even science sees this as a MIRACLE. The sex cells that the mother and father produce unite to form one cell, and this one cell divides, redivides, and continues multiple cycles of this process to create an entire human baby.

The process of making a baby is so complicated that Science has still not been able to decipher the complete process of conception in its terms. The *'Human Genome Project (1990*

– 2003)' has answered many questions. However, many areas of this highly specialised process are still unknown to humans.

Allow me to share some astonishing changes that happen to a woman's body during pregnancy:

1. The blood volume of a pregnant woman's body **increases by 40-50% of the average volume** to adapt to the requirement of carrying more oxygen to supply to the foetus.
2. A pregnant woman's **heart grows in size** to accommodate the increased blood volume and flow.
3. A pregnant woman's **vocal cords swell slightly** due to high levels of the reproductive hormones estrogen and progesterone during pregnancy. This can make the higher notes in her voice disappear, and specific lower notes may miraculously appear!
4. Usually, in the third trimester, **a pregnant woman's joints may loosen up to assist in childbirth**. This is the reason for the leg pain in advanced Pregnancy.
5. Pregnancy marks a woman's body with "**stretch marks**", usually on the breasts, abdomen, buttocks and thighs. A pregnant woman's belly may develop a **dark line (Linea Nigra; the "black line")** travelling from her belly button to her pubic area. **Dark, patchy spots (Chloasma)** may appear on a pregnant woman's face.
6. A pregnant woman's **skin stretches to accommodate the growing baby**.
7. A pregnant woman's **sense of smell is heightened** during pregnancy. An undesirable effect of this phenomenon is a dislike for particular places or foods, which may lead to

nausea or vomiting. However, an evolutionary mechanism prevents the mother from eating anything that might harm the unborn baby.

8. A pregnant woman's **breasts may start preparing and secreting breast milk as early as 14 weeks (the second trimester)** of pregnancy.
9. A pregnant woman's **hair and nail growth increase**. A key reason for this is the prenatal (the duration of pregnancy before childbirth) nutrients a pregnant woman consumes.
10. **Taking care of oral health** is especially important for pregnant women as gums swell during pregnancy and even bleed. This is a normal phenomenon of pregnancy arising from increased levels of estrogen and progesterone hormones in the body.
11. During pregnancy, a woman's **feet become more extended and broader**. This results from the hormone Relaxin loosening her bones and ligaments and the extra body weight pressing on the feet. In addition, increased fluid retention by a pregnant woman's body may cause her feet to swell. **A point of caution is that foot swelling may also result from a pregnancy complication and must be checked by a gynaecologist.**

Just stop reading. Give a kiss to your mother if she is there with you, and say, "Thank You." If she is not physically there with you, just give her a call, give her an online kiss, and say, "Thank You." If your mother has moved on like mine, just remember her pretty face, give her an energetic kiss and say "Thank You."

I want all of you women out there to realise at this moment how awesome you are. If you are a mother, feel the AWESOMENESS that you are. If you are yet to be a mother, feel super grateful for this INCREDIBLE ABILITY nature has blessed you with.

The kind of changes a pregnant woman's body undergoes is SUPERHUMAN. Even more miraculous is how her body returns to normal within a year of these awe-inspiring changes.

Put a hand on your heart and answer my question: "ISN'T CONCEPTION A POWER GIVEN TO WOMEN BY NATURE?"

My heart knows that your answer is an emphatic YES.

Aging Gracefully: Why Women Outlive Men

Go to any community in your neighbourhood, and you will always find more old women than old men.

A pathbreaking study done by the National Institute of Aging in Maryland, USA (*Guralnik et al., 2000*) made the following discoveries:

1. Almost all populations worldwide have a **considerably higher number of older women than men**.
2. In most countries, the **death rates of males are higher than those in females,** beginning from the womb and remaining higher throughout life.
3. This difference in men's and women's life expectancy **began in the 20th century**. A hundred years ago, the life expectancy of males and females was similar.

4. The **higher death rates in men of all ages understandably caused an increase in the number of women in the following age groups**. This results in a more significant number of women of advanced ages.
5. Biological factors implicated in the better life expectancy of women include **lower incidence and prevalence of coronary heart disease (CHD) and substantially higher survival rates in women for conditions such as pulmonary embolism, heart failure, and sepsis**.
6. One of the most prominent environmental factors bringing about the disparity in death rates between men and women in the 20th century was **men's increased use of tobacco-based products**. This began in the early 20th century and peaked in the mid-20th century. Men reached their peak smoking prevalence earlier than women and rose steeply throughout adolescence. Moreover, male smokers smoked more cigarettes per day and inhaled cigarette smoke more intensely than women.
7. Smoking is not the only factor causing higher male mortality. Male smokers also practice high-risk practices such as **alcohol intake**.

These findings point towards a phenomenon known as the "**female longevity advantage**".

Many of the practices followed by men, as mentioned in the findings above, such as smoking and alcoholism, though available to women today, are *not encouraged among them*. A woman smoking or drinking is looked down upon. Another aspect of this phenomenon is the social conditioning that men can smoke and drink. These practices are seen as manly. Don't believe me? Just watch a cigarette or alcohol ad on TV.

This is a classic example of patriarchal social norms negatively impacting men.

So, has nature hallmarked women to live long, fulfilling lives before and even long after birth?

The answer is a proud YES.

Double the X, Double the Benefits: How Two X Chromosomes Give Women an Edge

Women possess two X chromosomes, while men have one X and one Y chromosome.

Now, what the heck are X and Y chromosomes?

The X and Y chromosomes are two of the 23 pairs of chromosomes humans have in their cells. Chromosomes are thread-like structures that carry genetic information in the form of genes, which determine various traits and characteristics. The X and Y chromosomes are known as the "**sex chromosomes**", and they determine an individual's biological sex. The Y chromosome in males triggers the development of male reproductive organs during embryonic development. This is why **the father, who contains one X and one Y chromosome, determines whether the sex of the baby will be male (XY) or female (XX)**. Only the father can give the Y chromosome that determines the male sex of his son. The mother can only give one X chromosome to her child.

The X chromosome is more significant and has more genes than the Y chromosome. Some genes on the X chromosome play essential roles in various bodily functions, such as blood clotting and vision. In contrast, the Y chromosome contains fewer genes and is primarily responsible for developing male-specific traits.

About X-Chromosome Inactivation in Women:

One of the two X chromosomes a woman possesses is randomly inactivated during early embryonic development, a process known as X-chromosome inactivation. This means that some cells in a woman's body will express genes from one X chromosome while others will express genes from the other X chromosome.

Benefits of two X chromosomes in Women:

Several studies (*Arnold et al.; Libert et al.; Summers; Youness et al.; Niemi and Wu; Johnson et al., Nguyen and Disteche; Eskes and Haanen; and Smith and Warner*) have reported upon the natural advantage that the presence of two X-chromosomes gives women.

✓ One benefit is **genetic variation**. Since only one X chromosome is active in each cell, women have more genetic diversity than men, who only have one X chromosome. *This can increase the chances of survival in changing environments.*

✓ Another benefit is **protection against various diseases**. Some genes on the X chromosome are associated with certain conditions, such as haemophilia and Duchenne muscular dystrophy. In women, *the healthy X chromosome can compensate for the defective X chromosome by producing enough of the missing protein to prevent or reduce the severity of the disease.*

✓ Finally, X-chromosome inactivation **allows women to carry recessive genetic features without being affected**. For example, *if a woman has a recessive gene for a genetic disorder such as sickle cell anaemia or cystic fibrosis, but only one of her X chromosomes carries the gene, she is unlikely to be affected by the disease*. However, she can still pass the gene on to her children.

Chapter Summary:

1. While society considers women the "weaker sex", nature, in various ways, shows women to be the "resilient sex".
2. Several studies have shown that the female foetus has a better chance of surviving pregnancy up to a year after birth.
3. Male foetuses are susceptible to the negative effects of air pollution, maternal smoking and pregnancy complications.
4. During pregnancy, a woman's body undergoes tremendous changes to support the foetus.
5. Even more miraculous is how many women's bodies return to their regular sizes after pregnancy.
6. Females live longer than males in old age.
7. Certain social habits among men, like smoking and alcohol consumption, are the reasons for higher mortality rates in men than in women.
8. The presence of two X chromosomes in women benefits them in several ways.

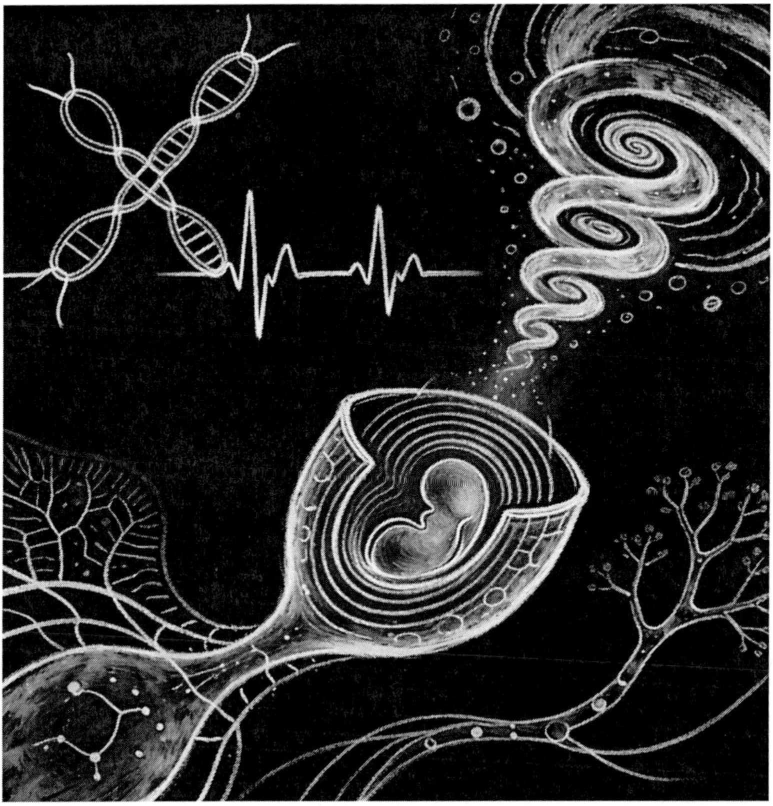

CHAPTER 3

THE POWER OF PERCEPTION: EXAMINING SOCIETY'S VIEWS ON WOMEN AND THEIR IMPACT

Gender Roles and Stereotypes

Rita's experience of Patriarchy in her childhood:

From a young age, Rita was acutely aware of how gender affected the opportunities and experiences available to her.

Rita was encouraged to pursue her education and develop her talents as a child. She excelled in school, earning top grades and demonstrating a natural aptitude for science and technology. However, as she got older, she noticed that her male peers were often given preferential treatment, with more opportunities and resources allocated to them simply because of their gender.

In the classroom, Rita was often overlooked or dismissed by male teachers who assumed she was not as capable or knowledgeable as her male classmates. Even when she excelled academically, she was often belittled or criticised for her opinions or ideas, simply because she was a girl.

Outside school, Rita faced similar challenges. She was discouraged from pursuing certain hobbies or interests, like sports or video games, deemed "unladylike" or inappropriate for girls. She was told that her primary role in life was to get married and have children and that her career aspirations were secondary to her domestic duties.

Despite these obstacles, however, Rita refused to be deterred. She continued to work hard and pursue her goals, determined to prove she was just as capable and deserving as her male peers. She found solace in support of other women in her family and community, who encouraged her to never give up on her dreams.

Have you ever heard one of these statements?

Or worse, have you ever been subjected to this kind of injustice?

"You are a girl; you cannot do this! Leave it to your brother!"

"What is the use of dreaming big? You will get married and go to another house when you grow up."

"What will you achieve by studying? Come, help me in the kitchen."

"You are a woman! You cannot run a business! Better learn to run a household or kitchen."

"Why are you learning maths? Girls are less intelligent than boys! All you need to know is kitchen measurements! That is the only math you'll ever need!"

"How can you drive a car? You are a woman! Don't you have any men in your house to drive the car?"

"Why are you travelling by yourself? You are either a woman or a girl."

"Oh my god! You are staying by yourself!"

"That girl is earning well and staying by herself! Her character is not good!"

The worst case is that boys and men are also subjected to bullying and gender-based verbal violence!

"Stop crying like a girl." (Statement directed at boys)

"Are you a girl?" (Statement directed at boys)?

"That girl is getting more marks than you! Are you an idiot?" (Statement directed at boys)

"That woman is earning more than you! Are you man enough?" (Statement directed at men)

"You are letting your wife drive/save money/invest by herself! You are not man enough!" (Statement directed at men!)

"You are helping your wife! Oh no! You are a henpecked husband!" (Statement directed at men!)

Society expects women to behave in certain ways and the social roles that they are expected to fulfil. This also includes how women are expected to talk, act and dress, the jobs they are supposed to do, and how they are expected to behave in relationships. Most of these expectations are often moulded by stereotypes and prejudices passed down by past generations. For instance, women are often expected to be emotional, nurturing, and submissive. In contrast, men are expected to be in control, self-confident and assertive.

Such expectations have a significant impact on women's lives. They limit the opportunities available to women and prevent them from attaining their full potential. For example, women are discouraged from pursuing careers in specific fields (e.g., automechanic, automotive driver, sports, and defence, etc.) or taking on leadership roles in society and the job sector because they are seen as too emotional or lacking in confidence.

Did You Know?

Let me tell you about Maitreyi, a remarkable woman who lived in ancient India. She was a renowned philosopher and scholar who lived roughly 3,000 years ago in the Vedic era.

Maitreyi was a pioneering female sage. She had a good education and was very interested in the nature of the cosmos, philosophy, and spirituality. Maitreyi pursued her love of study with perseverance and persistence despite being a woman in a patriarchal environment where women were frequently denied opportunities and education.

Maitreyi's contribution to the Upanishads, a group of Hindu intellectual literature, is one of her most notable accomplishments. With her spouse, the scholar Yajnavalkya, she had long philosophical talks, pushing him with her astute observations. Maitreyi's knowledge and awareness were recognised and respected by scholars and thinkers of her time. Her contributions to the field of philosophy have had a lasting impact, inspiring generations of scholars and thinkers in India and beyond.

Maitreyi's story reminds us of the essence of pursuing our passions and dreams, even in adversity. Her steadfast devotion and hunger for learning and philosophy inspire women and men alike to follow their paths, irrespective of how challenging they may seem.

Breaking Barriers: Tracing the Evolution of Women's Roles in Society.

Now, let us understand the social positioning of women down the ages and understand the roles, contributions, and challenges that they faced throughout history.

Ancient Women in Society: More Than Just Housewives

It is generally thought that women in the ancient world were predominantly confined to the household, and had limited opportunities to receive an education, do a job or interact in the public space. The role of women in ancient societies was indeed limited. However, there also were several exceptions. Ancient Egypt saw women holding important political and religious positions, with Cleopatra, Merneith and Hatshepsut serving as pharaohs (ruler of Egypt). While most women in ancient Greece were confined to their homes, some women, such as the philosopher Hypatia achieved outstanding academic success.

In ancient India, especially during the Pre-Vedic era, women faced no gender-based disparity. They enjoyed a social status equal to men. They were respected as the Mother Goddess ("*Devi*") and had the right to receive an education. The wives of sages could participate in spiritual activities, worshipping the religious deities and their husbands. The ancient Vedic texts saw women and men as the "two wheels of a cart".

Medieval Women in Society: From Home to Market

The Medieval period saw increased restrictions on women's roles, especially in Europe. Women were mostly confined to their homes, with very few women getting opportunities for education or exposure to public life. However, women played essential roles in their communities through their work at home, in agriculture, local markets, and trade. Women were involved in everything from cooking, cleaning, and selling goods at local markets. Their contributions were essential to their families' and communities' survival and well-being.

The later Vedic period saw a decline in equality and integrity among the genders in India. The social situation of women in Indian society nosedived during this time. The *Rigvedic*[8] morals of harmony and fairness between the genders were destroyed, depriving women of their right to study the Vedas and participate in any spiritual activities. Women became increasingly confined

---

[8] Rigvedic: Refers to something pertaining to Rigveda. The Rigveda is one of the oldest sacred texts of Hinduism, composed in ancient India around 1500 BCE. It contains hymns and prayers dedicated to various gods and goddesses.

to domestic life and were required to have an unquestionable devotion to their husbands.

Medieval India also witnessed the introduction of restrictive practices such as "*Purdah* (veil)" and honour-centric social femicide (woman killing) practices such as "*Sati*"[9] and "*Jauhar*"[10].

Women in the Renaissance and Enlightenment: New Opportunities and Challenges

The Renaissance and Enlightenment periods witnessed an expansion in women's opportunities once again. Women were increasingly able to receive an education and participate in the arts and sciences. However, they were still largely excluded from positions of power and authority. Most women continued to face significant discrimination and limitations. Highly educated women were often unable to pursue careers in the fields they chose and were instead expected to marry and have children.

The Renaissance period in India lasted between the 14th to the 17th century and saw significant transformation and progress in women's roles and status in society. While women in India during this period were still primarily confined to their homes, the era also saw the emergence of several notably exceptional women. Women from wealthy families could obtain an education and pursue interests outside their homes, such as music and arts. This era saw some important women poets and writers, such as Akka

[9] Widows were expected to self-immolate upon their husbands' deaths to save their honour.

[10] Women were expected to self-immolate to avoid capture or enslavement and consequent destruction of the family honour (as represented by women's bodies) by enemies.

Mahadevi and Mirabai. However, many women, particularly those from the lower castes, continued to experience significant social discrimination and subjugation during this time.

Women in the 19th and 20th Centuries: Breaking Down Barriers

The 19th and 20th centuries saw significant progress in women's rights and opportunities. Women obtained suffrage (the right to vote in elections) in several countries and began entering the workforce in substantial numbers. Numerous women's movements emerged, fighting for greater equality and the recognition of women's contributions to society. Women played vital roles during both World Wars I and II. During these wars, women not only served as nurses and ambulance drivers, but also served in factories and hospitals and volunteered for numerous organisations. The Civil Rights and the Women's Liberation Movement brought significant changes in women's social and legal status.

Indian women also saw significant transformation during this time, as they began to demolish barriers and fought for greater equality and rights. Indian women's suffrage movement gave them the right to vote in 1919. They also started entering the workforce more significantly, particularly in healthcare and education. However, women faced significant challenges and discrimination during this time, particularly gender-based violence and unequal pay. Despite such challenges, Indian women insisted on greater recognition and representation. Several women's rights organisations were founded in India during this time.

Contemporary Women's Issues: The Fight for Equality Continues

Even today, women continue facing challenges and discrimination in many parts of the world. Gender-based violence, limited access to education and healthcare, and unequal pay and opportunities at the workplace are some of the issues that continue to affect women's lives. However, women worldwide continue to fight for greater equality and recognition, building on the movements and the progress made by previous generations of women. From the #MeToo movement to the fight for reproductive rights, women increasingly stand up for their rights and demand change.

Like other women worldwide, Indian women face significant challenges regarding women's rights and gender equality. Gender-based violence, inclusive of sexual assault, domestic violence, and harassment, is one of the most pressing issues faced by Indian women today. Women in India also face significant barriers to education and employment, particularly in certain parts of the country. In 2025, the World Economic Forum (WEF) ranked India at the 131st position out of a total of 148 countries in its Global Gender Gap Index. Child marriage is another major issue facing women in India, which results in increased school dropout by girls and face early and often high-risk pregnancies, which may, in turn, lead to a high young mothers Mortality Rate and underweight babies.

Beyond Oppression: Examining the Complex Relationship between Women and Patriarchy

Patriarchy (Gr. *patriarkhēs*; "*the rule of the father*") is a social system that has existed for thousands of years and continues to shape how our society functions today. At its core, patriarchy is a system of authority and power that places men in positions of dominance over women. This is evident in many areas of society, from family dynamics and interpersonal relationships to politics and economics.

One of the significant ways in which patriarchy manifests itself is through the *gender-specific division of labour.* In patriarchal societies, while women are expected to care for the home and children, men are expected to work outside the home and provide for their families. This results in lower access to education, employment, and other opportunities for women, as well as women being unrecognised and poorly paid for the work that they do.

Patriarchy also *shapes gender roles and expectations, limiting how men and women can express themselves and interact.* According to patriarchal principles, men are expected to be dominant and aggressive, while women are expected to be submissive and caring. This, in turn, creates an environment in which men feel entitled to control and dominate women, and women are anticipated to accept this as the natural order of things.

Normalising gender-based violence, such as sexual assault, domestic abuse, and harassment, is another crucial aspect of patriarchy. In patriarchal societies, women are frequently held accountable for the violence they face rather than the culprits being blamed for it. This may lead to a victim-blaming culture that makes it challenging for women to come forward and ask for justice.

Despite the many challenges that patriarchy presents for women, there is also a *growing movement of feminist activism, an increase in the awareness of men and advocacy working on challenging and demolishing patriarchy*. By raising awareness about how patriarchy shapes our lives and advocating for gender equality and justice, we can create a society that is just and equitable towards everyone.

Women's contribution to Patriarchy:

Do you remember the iconic scene from the Bollywood movie Dangal in which Gita and Babita Phogat bash up two boys who harassed them? Do you remember what the boy's mother says?

Chal, Chhoriyon se pit gaya! (Come, you got bashed up by girls)

Why is it such a deplorable thing to be beaten or defeated by girls?

The underlying sentiment here is "Women are second-grade citizens. It is bad for them to be better than a boy or a man."

It is easy to think that patriarchy is a system solely created by men to oppress women. The truth is that **women have played a significant role in maintaining and contributing to the vicious cycle of patriarchy** throughout history.

The saddest part is that we women have bought into the principles of Patriarchy and believe it to be the absolute truth.

A prominent way women contribute to patriarchy is by *preserving traditional gender roles of men and women*. From a young age, women are taught by their female guardians (Grandmother, Mother and other female relatives) that they were born to fulfil domestic roles and take care of their families. At least one female relative also tells them that, to fulfill their role in the family better; women must sacrifice their dreams and career aspirations. By accepting and maintaining these patriarchal gender roles, women reinforce the idea that domestic work and caregiving are a woman's work, while paid work outside the home is a man's work. This strengthens gendered stereotypes and continues the idea that women are naturally suited to specific roles and tasks.

Another way women contribute to patriarchy is by *policing other women's behaviour and conduct.* Women are often expected to conform to the traditional gender roles and expectations assigned to them. Those who do not conform to these rigid definitions are often criticised or ostracised by other women. This can include anything, from dressing in a non-traditional way to pursuing careers or hobbies traditionally seen as suited for men. By policing other women's behaviour, women reinforce the idea that there is a "right" and "wrong" way to be a woman (the "Good Woman" and the "Bad Woman"). Women who deviate from traditional gender roles are somehow "less than" or not deserving of respect.

Women also contribute to patriarchy by *upholding harmful gender stereotypes.* This includes believing in and reinforcing ideas like women are more nurturing or emotional than men or that men are more logical or rational than women. Such stereotypes support the erroneous notion that men and women are fundamentally different and that one gender (male) is inherently better or more suited to specific tasks or roles.

Motherhood is the most responsible role for a woman. Children follow their mother's word for word for the first few years of their lives. What will you expect from a little boy brought up on such erroneous concepts of the differences between the genders and the idea that men are better than women by his mother, the person he loves and follows the most?

Is it entirely men's fault that they grow up believing women are second-class citizens?

Despite how women contribute to patriarchy, it's essential to note that women cannot be blamed for the oppression imposed upon them. **Patriarchy is a complex and profoundly ingrained system maintained and supplemented by both men and women**, and both genders must demolish it. By advocating for gender equality, challenging traditional gender roles and stereotypes and supporting each other, we can work towards creating a society that is truly equitable and just for all.

Factors that Influence Women's Perceptions of Abuse

Women's perceptions of abuse differ due to multiple factors, such as their cultural and social backgrounds, age, and education level. This chapter explores the different perceptions of abuse among women and the factors that influence these perceptions.

Cultural and Social Backgrounds

Women's perceptions of abuse can differ depending on their cultural and social backgrounds. For instance, in some cultures, women may perceive physical abuse as a sign of love or affection from their partners.

In contrast, physical abuse is seen as a severe violation of human rights in other cultures. Additionally, some societies view emotional abuse as usual in relationships, while others see it as mental torture.

Religion also plays a role in shaping women's perceptions of abuse. Some religious teachings promote the idea that women should be submissive to their husbands and that abuse is a form of discipline. Such instructions can make women more likely to accept abuse as part of their marital relationship.

Age and Education Level

Younger women may perceive abuse differently than older women. Younger women may view abuse as a regular part of a relationship and may not recognise the signs of abuse.

In contrast, older women may be more aware of the symptoms of abuse. They may have a lower tolerance for abusive behaviour. Education level can also influence women's perceptions of abuse. Women with higher levels of education may have more knowledge about abuse and its consequences. They may be more likely to seek help and support when experiencing abuse and less likely to accept it as part of a relationship.

Types of Abuse

Women's perceptions of abuse can also differ depending on their experience. For example, women who experience physical abuse may perceive it as more severe than emotional abuse.

However, women who experience emotional abuse may feel it is more challenging to recognise and address than physical abuse.

Financial abuse is another form of abuse that can affect women's perceptions of abuse. Women who are financially dependent on their partners may feel they have no choice but to accept abusive behaviour.

Additionally, women who have experienced financial abuse may view it as less severe than other forms of abuse.

In conclusion, women's perceptions of abuse can differ due to various factors, such as their cultural and social backgrounds, age, education level, and the type of abuse they experience. It is essential to understand these different perceptions to provide practical support and resources to women who are experiencing abuse. By acknowledging and addressing these perceptions, we can work towards ending abuse and creating a world where all women can live free from violence and oppression.

Unseen and Undervalued: Shedding Light on Women's Invisible Labor in the Home

Women have always been essential to domestic work and frequently shoulder more duties than men. Women contribute significantly to household chores. These contributions often go **unacknowledged and unappreciated.**

According to a United Nations study, women worldwide spend an average of 4.5 hours everyday on unpaid care tasks, including cleaning, cooking, and caring for children and elderly relatives. Conversely, men spend less than half of the time women spend at home. Women frequently have additional jobs outside the house besides their work at home, increasing their workload and stress levels.

The unequal allocation of household duties will have a detrimental effect on women's physical and mental health as well as their financial security. Also, it may reduce the opportunity for women to achieve their educational and professional ambitions.

Notwithstanding the difficulties, women still contribute significantly to home duties. Women are essential to maintaining the health of their families, communities, and society. As they offer emotional support and care to their loved ones, they frequently act as the glue that binds families together.

Recognising and appreciating the significant domestic labour done by women is crucial. We can advance gender equality and build a more just and equitable society for all by respecting and fostering women's contributions.

How women save billions and trillions of monies every year through unpaid household chores:

Depending on the country, the sort of employment, and the situation, women can save a wide range of money by taking on household chores. However, women's contributions to home duties can help families save a lot of money.

Cooking, cleaning, and caring for family members are just a few unpaid care tasks that Indian women perform on **average for 289 minutes (or around 5 hours) daily** (Time

Use Survey conducted by Ministry of Statistics and Programme Implementation, Government of India, 2024.). According to research by the National Sample Survey Office, this effort is expected to be worth roughly **Rs 19 lakh crore ($260 billion) yearly**, equivalent to 20% of the nation's GDP.

According to the Bureau of Labour Statistics, women in the USA spend an **average of 2.7 hours per day in 2024 on unpaid home tasks**, such as cooking, cleaning, and taking care of family members. Globally, this effort is projected to be worth trillions of dollars, with an **annual value of roughly $1.5 trillion** in the USA.

In India, eating out and getting takeout can be rather expensive. Therefore, women who prepare their meals save a lot of money. Moreover, using coupons, taking advantage of promotions, and purchasing in bulk are all ways that women who shop for groceries and other home items can save money.

Women who look after children and elderly relatives help families save money by reducing the need for costly daycare and nursing home care, which can amount to thousands of rupees annually. While women's contributions to household work help families save money, most of the time, these contributions go unappreciated and unnoticed. We can advance gender equality and build a more just and equitable society by appreciating and valuing women's contributions to household chores.

Chapter Summary:

1. Society expects women to behave in a certain way and fulfil specific responsibilities.
2. Women around the world, down the ages, have fought for their equality.
3. The social system of patriarchy considers men to be dominant over women.
4. Patriarchy shapes gender-specific division of labour as well as gender-specific roles and expectations.
5. Women play a significant role in maintaining and contributing to Patriarchy.
6. Men are also victims of patriarchy.
7. The domestic work done by women daily, which saves billions and trillions of money yearly, must be acknowledged more, mainly in households.

CHAPTER 4

CREATING SAFE SPACES: AN INTRODUCTION TO ENSURING WOMEN'S SAFETY IN THE HOME

Women's Safety begins at home

Rita had always thought of her family as loving and supportive, but as she grew older, she began to notice that her uncle would sometimes become angry and aggressive towards her.

At first, Rita thought it was just an occasional occurrence, but as time went on, she realised that it was much more serious than that. Her uncle would often yell and scream at her, and sometimes he would even hit her. Rita's mother would try to calm him down and make excuses for his behavior, but Rita could sense that something was seriously wrong.

As the violence at home continued, Rita began to feel scared and helpless. She didn't know what to do or who to turn to for help. She was worried for herself and her mother's inability to protect her from the abuse. ***(To be Continued)***

Safety is a fundamental right. Everyone must feel comfortable in their own homes since homes are our safe havens. Sadly, studies indicate, and our surroundings show us, that more women than men experience violence and abuse in their homes.

The various forms of physical, emotional, and sexual abuse that women may experience at home are introduced in this chapter. We will also discuss how violence affects women's daily lives, health, and general well-being. We also discuss domestic femicide, or the killing of women by intimate partners like spouses and lovers.

We hope that readers interested in learning more about this critical topic will find this chapter a helpful introduction and a valuable source of insight.

Painful yet True Stories: A few cases of gender-based violence against women at home, worldwide.

- In Colorado, USA, in 2018, a pregnant woman and her two daughters were killed by her husband, a man named Chris Watts, in cold blood.
- In Lahore, Pakistan, a 19-year-old Pakistani lady named Zeenat Rafiq was burned alive by her mother in 2016 for getting married without her family's consent.
- Karen Ristevski was murdered by her husband in Melbourne, Australia, in 2017.
- In Amman, Jordan, in 2019, Alaa Salah was fatally beaten by her husband.

- In 2018, Israeli settlers killed 16-year-old Palestinian Aisha Al-Rabi by throwing rocks at her car in the West Bank. They purportedly thought she was a Palestinian who had disgraced her family by dating a Jewish guy.
- In Madrid, Spain, in 2016, Jorge Chuecos killed his wife and two children.

The Domestic Violence Epidemic: Defining and Understanding Its Impact on Women

In a close relationship, such as a marriage or partnership, domestic violence refers to *a pattern of abusive behaviour used by one person to gain control and influence over another*. Abuse of any kind, including physical, sexual, emotional, and psychological abuse, can be committed. No matter your age, ethnicity, gender, or sexual orientation, domestic abuse can happen to anyone. Yet, it primarily impacts women.

Domestic violence has *a significant and long-lasting effect on the safety of women*. Physical harm, emotional anguish, and psychological suffering are possible side effects for women who encounter domestic abuse. As a result of the abuse, people could also endure financial difficulties and social isolation because they might be unable to work or participate in community activities.

Women's physical and mental health may be negatively impacted by domestic violence. *Anxiety, Depression, and Post Traumatic Stress Disorder (PTSD)* are more prevalent in women who have experienced domestic violence. As a result of the abuse, they could develop chronic pain and other medical concerns.

In addition to its negative consequences on women's physical and mental health, domestic violence can also have *an economic impact*. Women who experience domestic violence may lose their jobs or become unable to work due to the abuse. They can also be responsible for paying for their legal fees and medical costs related to the abuse.

Recognising how domestic violence affects women's safety and well-being is crucial, as is taking steps to prevent and address this issue. This entails offering assistance and support to victims of domestic abuse as well as educating the public and launching awareness campaigns to stop domestic violence before it starts. We can live in a safer and more just society if we band together to end domestic abuse.

Recognising the Signs: Understanding How Domestic Violence Manifests in Different Ways

Domestic abuse exists in many different forms, and not all of it is physical. It includes physical, sexual, emotional, psychological, and financial abuse. The most noticeable type of domestic violence is **physical assault**. It entails using physical force, such as hitting, kicking, punching, choking, or using weapons, to inflict hurt or injury. Physical harm, such as bruises, fractured bones, and internal ailments, can result from physical abuse.

Another form of domestic violence is **sexual abuse**, which includes any unwelcome sexual behaviour. This can involve forced sex acts, rape, sexual assault, and other types of sexual coercion. Physical harm from sexual abuse can also result in psychological and emotional damage.

One type of domestic violence that can be as harmful as physical abuse is **emotional abuse**. Name-calling, humiliation, isolation, and threats are just a few verbal and psychological strategies that can be used to manipulate and control the victim. Low self-esteem, anxiety, sadness, and other mental health problems can be brought on by emotional abuse.

Domestic violence, which entails restricting the victim's access to financial resources, is referred to as **financial abuse**. This may involve depriving the victim of funds, stopping them from working or making them account for every dollar they spend. Financial abuse can make a person dependent on others for support and vulnerable to additional abuse.

With **psychological violence**, a woman is harmed by being physically threatened with harm, having her belongings and pets destroyed, or isolating her from her support network (family, friends, school, and/or employment).It's critical to understand that domestic abuse can take many forms and that all these forms are harmful. It might be easier for victims and their loved ones to see abuse when it happens and seek assistance if they know the various types of domestic violence.

Preventing Domestic Violence: Why It Matters and What We Can Do

Domestic abuse can leave its victims with grave and prolonged consequences, including *bodily harm, emotional distress, and psychological harm*. The effects on families, communities, and society may also be extensive.

The safety and well-being of people, families, and communities depend on addressing and preventing domestic violence. It is a complicated problem requiring a multifaceted strategy that includes intervention, education, and raising awareness. It also entails holding abusers responsible for their acts and offering victims resources and assistance.

Overcoming the societal and cultural conventions that support domestic violence is one of the biggest hurdles in combating it. *Because domestic violence is frequently concealed from the public, victims may hesitate to seek assistance out of fear, shame, or stigma.* This is especially true in societies that value male dominance and forbid women from sharing their stories.

It takes a consistent, all-encompassing effort to address these underlying cultural problems. Together with fighting damaging social norms and advancing gender equality, this also entails educating and training those who work with domestic abuse victims and groups that support them.

Focusing on early intervention and prevention is equally necessary for preventing domestic violence. Education and resources are provided to help young people notice the warning signals of abusive conduct and comprehend healthy relationship dynamics. Also, it entails collaborating with law enforcement and other groups to spot domestic violence instances early on and act before they develop into more severe types of abuse.

The core causes of domestic violence must be addressed, and programmes and policies that protect victims and hold abusers accountable must be developed. Only then can domestic violence be prevented. This entails funding *victim assistance programmes, offering legal safeguards, and guaranteeing that offenders are prosecuted.*

Confronting and preventing domestic violence is crucial to building a society that is both safer and more just for all. It demands a concerted effort by people, groups, and governments worldwide and a persistent dedication to advancing gender equality, combating harmful social norms, and assisting abused people. We can make a society where domestic abuse is not tolerated. By banding together, everyone can live without fear of violence.

Femicide: Understanding the Horrific Reality of Gender-Based Killings

Let me quote a statistic that sends shivers down my spine whenever I remember it or read about femicide.

Every hour, five women around the world are killed by their families (Paternal and/ or Marital).

The practice of femicide is rooted in the animalistic tendencies of its perpetrators. Femicide doesn't distinguish between developed, developing and lesser-developed countries.

Shraddha Walkar's murder and her live-in partner's brutal attempts to get rid of her body are fresh in our minds. Pick up any newspaper, and you will find at least one femicide news report. The existence and prevalence of the practice of femicide is a massive blot on our "civilised" world.

Femicide is the term for **killing women and girls because of their gender**. It is a severe form of gender-based violence that reflects the unequal power relations between men and women in societies. Femicide occurs in many forms, including domestic violence, honour killings, sexual violence, and human trafficking. This chapter will explore the indicators, dynamics, statistics, prevention, and control of Femicide.

Indicators of Femicide:

Femicide is a complex phenomenon influenced by social, cultural, and economic factors. The following are some of the indicators of Femicide:

- **Gender inequality:** One of the primary indicators of Femicide is gender inequality. Women who live in societies with limited rights and opportunities are at a higher risk of being victims of Femicide.
- **Domestic violence:** Domestic violence is a leading cause of Femicide. Women in abusive relationships are at a significantly higher risk of being murdered by their partners.
- **Honor Killings**: Honor killings occur when a woman is killed by her family members because she has brought shame to the family. This could be because she has married outside her caste, had premarital sex, or refused to marry.
- **Sexual violence**: Sexual violence is another form of femicide. Women who are sexually assaulted are at a higher risk of being killed by their attackers.

Dynamics of Femicide:

Femicide is a complex phenomenon that involves multiple dynamics. The following are some of the dynamics of Femicide:

- Patriarchal norms: Patriarchal norms contribute to by reinforcing gender femicide inequality and violence against women. These norms support the idea that men have the right to control women and their bodies.
- Economic factors: Economic factors, such as poverty and unemployment, can also contribute to femicide. Women economically dependent on men are at a higher risk of being murdered by their partners.
- Lack of access to justice: Women victims of femicide often face barriers when seeking justice. These barriers include limited access to legal representation, fear of reprisals, and lack of trust in the justice system.

Statistics on Femicide:

Femicide is a global issue that affects women from all walks of life. The following are some statistics on Femicide:

- As per a UNODC-UN Women-World Health Organization study(2024), an estimated 50,000 women and girls around the world were killed by a family member.
- In India, over 6,100 women were killed in 2023 in dowry-related incidents.
- In the United States, three women are killed by their partners daily.

Prevention and Control of Femicide:

Prevention and control of Femicide require a comprehensive approach that addresses the underlying causes and risk factors. The following are some tips for the prevention and control of Femicide:

- ✓ **Educate the public:** Education is a crucial component of preventing femicide. Public education campaigns can help raise awareness about the issue and promote gender equality.
- ✓ **Strengthen laws and policies:** Governments should enact laws and policies that protect women from violence and hold perpetrators accountable for their actions.
- ✓ **Provide support services:** Women who are victims of femicide need access to support services, including counselling, legal aid, and safe shelters.
- ✓ **Engage men and boys:** Men and boys play a critical role in preventing femicide. Programs that engage men and boys in the fight against gender-based violence can help change social norms and behaviours.

The following are some examples of femicide prevention and control programs:

1. The "**Ni Una Menos**" movement in Latin America: This is a feminist movement that began in Argentina in 2015 to protest gender-based violence and Femicide. It has since spread to other countries in the region, leading to significant policy changes to prevent femicide.
2. The "**Sisters in Solidarity**" program in Papua New Guinea: This program brings together women's groups

and community leaders to raise awareness about violence against women and promote gender equality. It has led to the establishment of safe houses for women and improved access to justice for survivors.

3. The campaign on "**16 Days of Activism against Gender-Based Violence**": This is an annual campaign that takes place from 25th November (International day for the elimination of violence against women) to 10th December (Human Rights Day) to raise awareness and mobilise action to prevent gender-based violence.
4. The "**He For She**" campaign by UN Women: This campaign calls on men and boys to stand up against gender-based violence and promote gender equality. It has gained significant traction globally, with millions of men and boys pledging to support the cause.
5. The "**White Ribbon Campaign**" in Canada: This campaign encourages men and boys to speak out against gender-based violence and take action to prevent it. It has led to the establishment of a national action plan to prevent violence against girls and women.
6. The "**National Plan to reduce violence against women and their children**" in Australia: This plan was launched in 2010 and aims to prevent and respond to violence against women and children through a range of initiatives, including education, support services, and legal reforms.
7. The "**One Stop Crisis Center**" in Bangladesh: This centre provides survivors of gender-based violence access to medical care, counselling, legal aid, and other support services in a

single location. It has helped to improve access to justice and support for survivors.

8. The "**Community Policing**" program in South Africa: This program trains police officers to work with communities to prevent and respond to gender-based violence. It has led to increased reporting of violence and improved access to justice for survivors.
9. The "**Gender and Development Network**" in the United Kingdom: This network brings together NGOs and other organisations to promote gender equality and prevent gender-based violence. It has led to policy changes and improved support services for survivors.
10. The "**Jalisco Violeta**" program in Mexico: This program aims to prevent femicide and gender-based violence through education, awareness-raising, and legal reforms. It has led to establishment of a femicide alert system and improved support services for survivors.
11. The "**Safe Cities**" program in several cities worldwide aims to make public spaces safer for women and girls by improving lighting, transportation, and police response.
12. The "**Girl Power**" program in Uganda empowers young girls to speak out against violence. It promotes education and economic empowerment for girls.
13. The "**Protection Against Domestic Violence Act**" in Nepal criminalises domestic violence and provides women with protection orders, counselling, and legal aid.
14. The "**Bell Bajao**" campaign in India encourages men and boys to intervene when they witness violence against women and girls.

Chapter Summary:

The pattern of abusive behavior used to dominate another person is known as domestic violence.

1. Domestic violence has long-term and varied effects on its victims.
2. Domestic violence can be seen and experienced in physical, sexual, emotional, psychological, and financial abuse.
3. Domestic violence affects women and children, families, communities, and society.
4. Domestic violence and its underlying causes can be challenged and prevented only by the concerted efforts of people, groups and governments worldwide.
5. Femicide (the murder of women and girls) is rooted in societal and cultural norms that disrespect and abuse women and girls.
6. Femicide can be prevented and responded to through a multifaceted strategy addressing factors contributing to gender-based violence.

CHAPTER 5

BREAKING THE SILENCE: SHEDDING LIGHT ON THE REALITIES OF DOMESTIC VIOLENCE

Sexual Violence at Home

How did Rita realise that what her uncle was doing was wrong?

Rita had learned about healthy relationships and the signs of abuse from school and her friends. She remembered her School Counselor teaching them that it was never okay for someone to use violence or force in a relationship, and that it is important to speak out against such behaviors.

Consequently, Rita realized that the violence that she experienced at home was wrong because she could see the fear building up within her when her uncle entered their house the way he affected her whole family. She saw how her uncle would yell and scream at herself, and sometimes even hit her. Rita understood that this was not a healthy or loving relationship, and that her Uncle's behavior was not acceptable. **(To be continued)**

Despite the prevalence of domestic violence, many women find it challenging to recognise the signs and seek help. Victims often feel ashamed or afraid to speak out and may believe that they are somehow responsible for the abuse they are experiencing. Abusers, meanwhile, may use a range of tactics to deny, justify, or minimise their behaviour, making it even harder for victims to identify what is happening to them.

This chapter will explore how to recognise the warning signs of abuse, its impacts on the victims, and the dynamics underlying this phenomenon. By understanding the complexities of domestic violence and learning how to recognise and respond to it, we can help create safer, healthier homes and communities for everyone.

A story of resilience and action:

The year 2016, Tucson, Arizona, USA: A woman named Tabitha was a victim of domestic violence by her partner, Mark. He physically and emotionally abused her for years, and she had lost all hope of escaping from the abusive relationship.

One day, Tabitha went to a gas station, and the attendant noticed her injuries and called the police. The police came to her aid and helped her get out of the abusive relationship. Tabitha was able to receive the necessary medical treatment and counselling, and she was able to rebuild her life free from violence.

This incident highlights the importance of recognising the signs of domestic violence and seeking help before it's too late. It also emphasises the role of community members and law enforcement in identifying and addressing domestic violence.

Spotting the Signs: How to Identify Domestic Violence

Suppose you suspect you or someone you know may be experiencing domestic violence. In that case, knowing the signs and taking action to protect yourself and/ or your loved ones is essential.

Physical Indicators of Domestic Violence Against Women

Physical abuse is one of the most visible forms of domestic violence against women and often leaves behind physical evidence. Some biological indicators of domestic violence against women include:

- Bruises, cuts, or scratches
- Broken bones or fractures
- Head injuries or concussions
- Internal injuries or organ damage
- Bite marks or strangulation marks
- Burns or scalds
- Marks from being hit with an object, such as a belt or a bat
- Injuries that are inconsistent with the explanation given or injuries that are not explained at all.

It's important to note that physical abuse is not always visible. Women experiencing domestic violence may try to hide their injuries or make excuses for them. They may also wear clothing that covers their injuries or avoid social situations.

Emotional Indicators of Domestic Violence Against Women

Emotional abuse is another form of domestic violence against women, and it can be just as damaging as physical abuse. Emotional abuse can include:

- Verbal abuse, such as name-calling, insults, or threats
- Constant criticism or put-downs
- Isolation from friends and family
- Controlling behaviour, such as monitoring phone calls or internet use
- Withholding affection or emotional support
- Blaming the victim for the abuse
- Gaslighting, which is when the abuser manipulates the victim into questioning their own sanity or perception of reality

Emotional abuse can be challenging to detect, as it often happens behind closed doors. Women who are experiencing emotional abuse may feel isolated, helpless, or ashamed. They may also blame themselves for the misuse or believe they deserve it.

Behavioural Indicators of Domestic Violence Against Women

Domestic violence against women can also manifest in behavioral changes. Some behavioral indicators of domestic violence against women include:

- Changes in sleep patterns, such as oversleeping or insomnia.

- Changes in eating habits, such as loss of appetite or overeating
- Increased use of drugs or alcohol
- Withdrawal from social activities or hobbies
- Decreased performance at work or school
- Avoiding eye contact or appearing nervous or fearful
- Attempts to cover up injuries or bruises
- Suicidal thoughts or attempts

These behavioural changes can result from physical or emotional abuse or both. Women experiencing domestic violence may feel overwhelmed or unable to cope with their situation, which can lead to changes in behaviour.

Recognising the Red Flags: Identifying 54 Signs of Domestic Violence

No one is born an abuser. Our upbringing and social exposure around us shape our formative years. What I am trying to drive home here is that a spouse does not become abusive overnight. The development of oddities and behaviour shifts can be observed over time in the change from ordinary to vicious within an individual. These oddities and behaviour shifts are known as **red flags of gender-based violence.**

Many red flags may indicate the presence of domestic violence in a relationship. These red flags include physical abuse, emotional abuse, and controlling behaviour. It's important to recognise these signs and take action to protect yourself or your loved ones.

Here are 54 red flags indicative of gender-based violence at home:

1. Extreme jealousy or possessiveness.
2. Attempts to control or limit access to finances.
3. Monitoring phone or internet use.
4. Dictating what a partner can wear or who they can talk to.
5. Insults, put-downs, and constant criticism.
6. Threats of violence or harm to a partner, children, or pets.
7. Threatening gestures, such as punching walls or throwing objects.
8. Constantly checking up on a partner's whereabouts.
9. Using physical force during arguments.
10. Blaming a partner for their own abusive behaviour.
11. Withholding affection or emotional support as a form of punishment.
12. Forcing a partner to engage in sexual acts against their will.
13. Using alcohol or drugs to excuse abusive behaviour.
14. Refusing to let a partner leave home or go out without permission.
15. Using intimidation or threats to isolate a partner from family and friends.
16. Engaging in stalking behaviour, such as following a partner or appearing unexpectedly.
17. Minimising or denying abusive behaviour.
18. Engaging in controlling or violent behaviour during pregnancy.
19. Threatening to harm or kill oneself if a partner leaves.
20. Using children as leverage or threatening to break them to control a partner.
21. Forcing a partner to have a child against their will.
22. Pressuring a partner to get pregnant.

23. Using religion or culture to justify abusive behaviour.
24. Dismissing a partner's opinions or feelings.
25. Refusing to take responsibility for one's own actions.
26. Gaslighting or manipulating a partner to question their own reality.
27. Refusing to allow a partner to work or go to school.
28. Forcing a partner to quit their job or drop out of school.
29. Using threats or violence to prevent a partner from leaving.
30. Making derogatory comments about a partner's race, ethnicity, or cultural background.
31. Forcing a partner to conform to gender roles or expectations.
32. Denying a partner access to healthcare or necessary medical treatment.
33. Using a partner's immigration status as leverage or threatening deportation.
34. Withholding food or basic needs as a form of punishment.
35. Pressuring a partner to engage in risky or illegal behaviour.
36. Refusing to use contraception or condoms, or sabotaging birth control.
37. Forcing a partner to engage in non-consensual BDSM or other sexual practices.
38. Refusing to allow a partner access to their own personal items or property.
39. Making threats or engaging in violence towards a partner's family or friends.
40. Using blackmail or extortion to control a partner.
41. Restricting a partner's access to transportation or communication devices.
42. Refusing to allow a partner to leave the house or room.

43. Engaging in financial abuse, such as stealing a partner's money or opening credit cards in their name.
44. Threatening to harm or kill pets or other animals.
45. Forcing a partner to choose between them and their family or friends.
46. Using physical violence to control a partner's behaviour.
47. Forcing a partner to use drugs or alcohol.
48. Threatening to reveal embarrassing or damaging information about a partner.
49. Engaging in revenge porn or sharing intimate photos without a partner's consent.
50. Refusing to allow a partner to have any privacy.
51. Controlling or limiting a partner's access to healthcare or mental health treatment.
52. Refusing to listen to a partner's concerns or needs.
53. Insisting on having access to a partner's phone or email.
54. Forcing a partner to have sex.

Recognising the red flags for women and girls and taking action to address gender-based violence is crucial. By being aware of these signs, you can help yourself, or someone you know escapes a dangerous situation and seek the help they need to move forward.

The Devastating Toll of Domestic Violence: Physical and Mental Health Consequences for Victims

The impact of domestic violence on women's physical and mental health can be significant and long-lasting. In this chapter, we will explore domestic violence's physical and psychological health effects on women.

Physical Health Effects of Domestic Violence

Domestic violence can have a range of physical health effects on women, including:

- Injuries: Women who experience domestic violence are at increased risk of physical injuries, such as bruises, cuts, broken bones, and head injuries.
- Chronic pain: Women who experience domestic violence may develop chronic pain as a result of their injuries or ongoing abuse.
- Gynecological problems: Women who experience domestic violence may be at increased risk of gynaecological issues, such as sexually transmitted infections, pelvic pain, and menstrual disorders.
- Pregnancy complications: Women who experience domestic violence during pregnancy may be at increased risk of complications, such as preterm birth, low birth weight, and miscarriage.
- Chronic health conditions: Women who experience domestic violence may be at increased risk of developing chronic health conditions, such as heart disease, arthritis, and asthma.

Mental Health Effects of Domestic Violence

The mental health effects of domestic violence can be just as devastating as the physical effects. Women who experience domestic violence are at increased risk of:

- **Depression**: Women who experience domestic violence may feel sad, hopeless, and worthless.
- **Anxiety**: Women who experience domestic violence may feel nervous, fearful, and on edge.
- **Post-traumatic stress disorder (PTSD)**: Women who experience domestic violence may develop PTSD. This condition can occur after a person witnesses or experiences a traumatic event.
- **Substance abuse**: Women who experience domestic violence may develop a drug or alcohol habit to cope with their abuse.
- **Suicidal thoughts and behaviour**: Women who experience domestic violence may feel hopeless and may contemplate or attempt suicide.

Social and Economic Effects of Domestic Violence

In addition to these mental health effects, women who experience domestic violence may also experience social and economic consequences such as:

- **Isolation**: Women who experience domestic violence may be isolated from their family and friends, making it challenging to seek help and support.
- **Job loss**: Women who experience domestic violence may have to miss work due to injuries or other reasons related to the abuse. They may also lose their jobs if their abuser interferes with their employment, or they must move to escape the abuse.
- **Financial insecurity**: Women who experience domestic violence may have limited access to financial resources, as their abuser may control their finances or prevent them from

working. This can make paying for basic needs such as shelter, food and medical care difficult.

- **Housing instability**: Women who experience domestic violence may have to leave their homes to escape the abuse. This can make it challenging to find safe and stable housing, mainly if they have limited financial resources or if they have children.
- **Stigma and discrimination**: Women who experience domestic violence may experience stigma and discrimination from others who blame them for the abuse or do not believe their stories.

Understanding Domestic Violence Dynamics: Power, Control, Manipulation, and Isolation

This chapter will explore the dynamics of domestic violence against women, including power and control, manipulation, and isolation. We will also provide examples of these dynamics to help illustrate their impact on women's lives.

Power and Control

At the heart of domestic violence against women is the issue of power and control. Abusers use violence to control their victims and maintain power over them. This can take many forms, including physical, sexual, emotional, and financial abuse.

- **Physical abuse** is perhaps the most visible form of domestic violence. Physical abuse is often used to intimidate women and make them feel powerless.
- **Sexual abuse** is another form of domestic violence often used to exert power and control over women. Abusers may use sex

to punish or reward their victims or exercise control over their bodies and sexuality.

- **Emotional abuse** is a more subtle form of domestic violence that can be difficult to recognise. It involves using words, gestures, and actions to make a woman feel worthless, powerless and controlled.
- **Financial abuse** is another way abusers can maintain power and control over women. By controlling a woman's finances, abusers can keep them dependent and prevent them from leaving the relationship.

Example: Mary is a stay-at-home mother of two children. Her husband, John, works full-time and is the sole provider for the family. John controls all the finances and gives Mary an allowance each week. He uses this to hold her and prevent her from leaving the relationship.

Manipulation

Manipulation is another key dynamic in domestic violence against women. Abusers often use manipulation to maintain control over their victims and make them feel powerless. This can take many forms, including gaslighting, blaming, and minimising the abuse.

- **Gaslighting** is a form of manipulation that makes a woman doubt her perceptions and reality. Abusers may deny the abuse or claim that the victim exaggerates or makes things up. This can leave the victim feeling confused, helpless, and unsure of themselves.
- **Blaming** is another form of manipulation that abusers use to deflect responsibility for their actions. They may blame the

victim for provoking the abuse or claim they were stressed or had too much to drink. This can leave the victim feeling guilty and responsible for the misuse, even though it is not their fault.

- **Minimising the abuse** is another way that abusers can manipulate their victims. They may claim that the abuse is not that bad or just a normal part of a relationship. This can make the victim feel like they are overreacting or being overly sensitive.

Example: Sarah's husband, Tom, is verbally abusive towards her. He often calls her names and belittles her in front of their friends and family. When Sarah confronts him about his behaviour, he denies doing anything wrong and claims she overreacts. He also tells her that she is lucky to have him and that no one else would put up with her.

Isolation

Isolation is the final dynamic in domestic violence against women. It involves controlling women's access to people, resources, and information. Abusers may isolate their victims from friends and family, restrict their access to transportation, and prevent them from working or going to school. By doing this, abusers can limit their victim's ability to seek help or leave the relationship.

Example: Avantika's husband, Anand, is extremely jealous and controlling. He doesn't like her spending time with friends or family, and he often makes her cancel plans at the last minute. He has also prevented her from getting a job, claiming he doesn't want her to be around other men. As a result, Amanda has become increasingly isolated and has few people to turn to for help or support.

Chapter Summary:

1. Knowledge of the indicators of domestic violence is the first step towards protecting yourself and/ or your loved ones.
2. Domestic violence can be identified through physical, emotional and behavioural indicators.
3. Domestic violence has a long-lasting impact on the victim's physical, mental, social and emotional health.
4. Domestic violence is based on the dynamics of power and control, manipulation and isolation of the victims.

CHAPTER 6

CREATING A PLAN FOR SAFETY: UNDERSTANDING THE IMPORTANCE OF SAFETY PLANNING

Self-Defence and Personal Empowerment

<u>Rita's Safety Plan:</u>

Rita's uncle's behavior had escalated to the point where Rita was genuinely scared of him. He had started yelling at her more frequently, and she had even seen him hit her younger brother when he came to defend Rita.

Rita knew that she needed to take action to protect herself and her family, but she didn't know where to start. She talked to a counsellor at her school, and they helped her create a safety plan. Here are some of the steps they took:

- ✓ Identify safe places: *Rita and her counsellor made a list of safe places she could go if she felt threatened or scared. Those included her friend's house, a neighbor's house, and the local library.*
- ✓ Emergency contacts: *Rita made a list of emergency contacts, including the police, a trusted family member, and her counsellor's phone number.*
- ✓ Escape routes: *Rita and her counsellor went over different escape routes from her house in case of an emergency. They identified the best exits and made sure that they were clear and easy to access.*
- ✓ Code word: *Rita and her counsellor came up with a code word that she could use to let her family and friends know that she was in danger without tipping off her uncle.*
- ✓ Safety at school: *Rita's counselor talked to her teachers and the school resource officer about her situation. They put a safety plan in place at school, including a plan for Rita to quickly and quietly leave class if she felt threatened.*
- ✓ Document incidents: *Rita kept a journal of all the incidents involving her uncle, including the date, time, and a brief description of what happened. This helped her keep track of any patterns of abuse and provided evidence if she needed to involve the police.*
- ✓ Trust her instincts: *Finally, Rita's counsellor stressed the importance of trusting her instincts. If she felt unsafe, she should leave the situation immediately and seek help.*

*Creating a safety plan was an important step for Rita in protecting herself and her family from her abusive uncle.(***To be continued)**

To protect themselves from violence, women must have a safety plan.

Safety planning is a proactive process that involves identifying potential risks and developing strategies to minimise them. It can be done by anyone at risk of violence, including women currently experiencing abuse, those who have left an abusive relationship, and those concerned about their safety in the future.

This chapter will explore the basics of safety planning for gender-based violence against women. We will discuss the importance of safety planning, the critical components of a safety plan, and some tips for creating an effective strategy.

By taking the time to develop a safety plan, women can take control of their situation and increase their chances of staying safe. Whether they are still in an abusive relationship or have left, a safety plan can provide a roadmap for visiting safely and minimising the risk of violence.

Did you know:

Here are some real-life examples of safety planning for gender-based violence against women in India:

1. <u>One-Stop Centers:</u> One-Stop Centers (OSCs) have been established across India to provide survivors of gender-based violence with a safe space to access medical, legal, and counselling services. These centres are equipped with trained professionals who can help survivors develop safety plans, provide emergency assistance, and connect them with resources in their community. Survivors can access these services free

of charge and are provided with a safe space to share their experiences without any fear of judgment or retribution.

2. Self-defence classes: In recent years, self-defence classes have become increasingly popular in India as a way for women to protect themselves from violence. These classes teach women how to defend themselves physically and mentally in dangerous situations. They also allow women to connect with others who have experienced similar problems and share strategies for staying safe.
3. Mobile apps: Several mobile apps have been developed in India to help women stay safe and access resources in an emergency. One such app is the **Himmat** app, developed by the Delhi Police, which allows women to send out an SOS signal to the police in case of danger. Another app, **Safetipin**, provides users with information on the safety of different areas in their city based on factors such as lighting, visibility, and crowds.

Preparing for the Worst: Creating an Emergency Safety Plan

A safety plan in place is a crucial resource for women experiencing violence at home to stay safe and protect themselves and their children.

Identifying a Safe Place to Go:

The first step in creating a safety plan is identifying a safe place to go in an emergency. Here are some examples of safe places women can go to seek refuge and protection:

✓ **Domestic Violence Shelters**: Domestic violence shelters are safe havens for women and children fleeing abusive relationships. These shelters offer temporary housing, food, and necessities such as clothing and toiletries. They also provide counselling, legal advocacy, and other support services to help women rebuild their lives.

For example, the Majlis Manch shelter in Mumbai, India, provides safe accommodation, legal and counselling services, and assistance finding employment for women who have experienced gender-based violence.

✓ **Family or Friends**: Women can also turn to trusted family members or friends for temporary shelter. Identifying individuals who are supportive and willing to provide a safe place to stay is essential. It is also crucial to ensure that the location is not known to the abuser and that the individual is not at risk of harming themselves.

For instance, a woman experiencing abuse from her partner may contact her sister, who lives in a different city, for temporary shelter.

✓ **Hotel or Motel**: In some cases, women may choose to stay in a hotel or motel for a short period. It is crucial to select a safe and secure location and ensure that the abuser does not have access to the room or know the area.

For example, a woman travelling to a different city for work may stay in a hotel or motel for a few nights to avoid returning to an abusive partner.

✓ **Public Places**: In emergencies, women can seek refuge in public places such as a police station, hospital, or fire department.

These locations have trained professionals who can provide immediate assistance and help connect women with resources and services.

For instance, a woman being followed or harassed by an abuser can seek help at a nearby police station or hospital to ensure her safety.

Creating a Communication Plan:

Communication is an integral part of a safety plan. Women should create a plan for how they will communicate with trusted individuals in case of an emergency. This could include having a code word or phrase signalling a trusted person who needs help. It could also involve setting up a system for regular check-ins with friends or family to ensure the woman is safe. Here are some examples of ways to create a communication plan:

- ✓ **Establish a Code Word or Signal:** Women can establish a code word or signal with trusted individuals to indicate that they are in danger and need help. This can be a word or phrase that is easy to remember and not likely to be used in regular conversation.

For example, a woman can establish a code word with her sister to indicate that she is in danger and needs help. Suppose the sister receives a text message containing the code word. In that case, she will know to call the police or take other appropriate action.

- ✓ **Use a Safety App:** There are many safety apps available that can be used to alert trusted individuals or emergency services in case of an emergency. These apps can include GPS tracking, panic buttons, and automatic calls to emergency services.

For instance, the Satark is a 'Made in India' personal safety app that lets you send an SOS in seconds, instantly alerting your trusted contacts with your live GPS location. It is quick to set up and designed for women and families, so that you can move through daily life with greater confidence and peace of mind.

✓ **Keep a List of Emergency Contacts**: Women should keep a list of emergency contacts in a safe and accessible location. This list should include the phone numbers of trusted family members, friends, and professionals such as doctors, counsellors, and lawyers.

For example, a woman can keep a list of emergency contacts in her purse or wallet to access it quickly in an emergency.

✓ **Use Social Media Safely:** Women can use social media platforms to contact trusted individuals for help. It is vital to ensure that the abuser does not have access to the woman's social media accounts or know her passwords.

For instance, a woman can send a private message to a trusted friend on social media to indicate that she is in danger and needs help.

Gathering Important Documents and Items

In addition to identifying a safe place to go and creating a communication plan, it is also crucial for women to gather important documents and items in case of an emergency. Here are some examples of documents and items that women should consider gathering:

✓ **Identification**: Women should gather essential identification documents such as passports, driver's licenses, and birth certificates. These documents are necessary to establish identity and access to healthcare and government benefits.

For example, a woman fleeing an abusive relationship should gather her passport and other identification documents to ensure she can travel and access services.

✓ **Financial Documents**: Women should gather critical financial documents such as bank account information, credit card information, and mortgage or lease agreements. These documents are necessary for accessing financial resources and establishing financial independence.

For instance, a woman leaving an abusive partner should gather financial documents to ensure she can access funds and establish her financial stability.

✓ **Medical Records**: Women should gather vital medical records such as immunisation records, medication lists, and allergy information. These records are necessary for accessing medical care and ensuring continuity of care.

For example, a woman fleeing an abusive relationship should gather her medical records to access necessary medical care and medications.

✓ **Items of Necessity**: Women should gather necessary items such as clothing, toiletries, and medications. Collecting sentimental items, such as family photographs and jewellery, is also vital.

For instance, a woman fleeing an abusive relationship should gather necessary items such as clothing, toiletries, and sentimental items that provide comfort and support.

Women need to keep these documents and items in a safe and accessible location. Women should also consider making copies of important documents and keeping them separate if the originals are lost or destroyed. Women should also update the list of papers and items regularly to ensure that it is current and accurate.

Creating a Personalised Safety Plan

Creating a personalised safety plan is crucial for women experiencing gender-based violence. A customised safety plan outlines women's steps to protect themselves and their children from harm. Here are some examples of how to create a personalised safety plan:

✓ **Assess Risk**: Women should assess the level of risk in their situation by considering the severity and frequency of the abuse. This helps determine what steps should be taken in the safety plan.

For example, suppose the abuse escalates and becomes more frequent. In that case, the woman may need to take more drastic measures to ensure her safety.

✓ **Identify Triggers**: Women should identify triggers that may escalate the violence and avoid these triggers as much as possible.

For instance, if the abuser is triggered by alcohol, the woman may need to avoid alcohol or ensure that she is not around the abuser when he drinks.

✓ **Create a Safety Plan for Children**: If the woman has children, she should create a separate safety plan. This may involve identifying a safe place for them to go in an emergency and teaching them what to do.

For example, the woman can teach her children to call the police or a trusted family member in an emergency and establish a code word or signal indicating they are in danger.

✓ **Establish Boundaries**: Women should establish clear boundaries with the abuser and communicate these boundaries clearly. This may involve setting limits on contact, such as blocking the abuser's phone number or social media accounts.

✓ **Practice Self-Care**: Women should prioritise self-care and practice techniques that promote mental and emotional well-being. This may involve practising meditation, journaling, or seeking professional counselling. For example, the woman can create a self-care routine that includes daily exercise, healthy eating, and meditation to help manage stress and promote well-being.

It is crucial for women to regularly review and update their safety plans as needed. Women should also share their safety plan with trusted individuals, such as family members, friends, and counsellors, to ensure they are aware of the procedure and can support them in an emergency.

Enlisting the Help of a Professional

When creating a safety plan, it can be helpful for women experiencing gender-based violence to enlist the help of a professional. A professional can provide support, resources, and guidance to help women navigate creating a safety plan. Here are some examples of professionals who can assist with creating a safety plan:

- **Domestic Violence Shelter Staff:** Staff at domestic violence shelters are trained to provide support and resources to women experiencing gender-based violence. They can assist with creating a safety plan, access legal assistance and counselling resources, and connect women with community support.
- **Counsellors or Therapists**: Counselors or therapists can provide emotional support and guidance to women experiencing gender-based violence. They can also assist with creating a safety plan and provide strategies for managing stress and trauma.
- **Legal Advocates**: Legal advocates can support and guide women experiencing gender-based violence. They can assist with obtaining restraining orders, filing for divorce or custody, and accessing resources such as legal aid.
- **Medical Professionals**: Medical professionals can provide support and resources to women experiencing gender-based violence. They can assist with documenting injuries, providing

medical care and referrals, and connecting women with community support.

For example, a woman experiencing gender-based violence can enlist the help of a domestic violence shelter staff member to assist with creating a safety plan. The staff member can provide resources and support, such as connecting the woman with legal assistance and counselling services. Additionally, the woman can enlist the help of a counsellor or therapist to provide emotional support and guidance throughout the process.

Creating a safety plan is essential in protecting oneself from gender-based violence. Every woman should know that she is not alone and that resources are available to help her stay safe. By identifying a safe place to go, creating a communication plan, and gathering important documents and items, women can take control of their safety and protect themselves and their children.

Staying Safe in an Abusive Relationship: Tips for Seeking Help and Support

If you are in an abusive relationship, it can be difficult to know what steps to take to protect yourself. Here are some tips for staying safe while in an abusive relationship, including how to get help and support.

- ✓ **Develop a Safety Plan:** Creating a safety plan can help you to identify potential dangers and plan to keep yourself safe. This can include identifying a safe place to go, creating a communication plan, and gathering important documents and items.

For example, you can identify a friend or family member who you can stay with in case of an emergency. You can also create a code word or phrase to let someone know that you are in danger without tipping off your abuser. Additionally, you can gather important documents such as identification, financial records, and medical records and keep them in a safe place.

✓ **Seek Support:** It can be difficult to leave an abusive relationship on your own. Seek support from friends, family, or a professional who can help you through the process. You can also reach out to organizations that provide support and resources to individuals experiencing domestic violence.

For example, you can reach out to a domestic violence hotline for support and information on resources in your area. You can also seek counseling or therapy to help you process the trauma and emotional impact of the abuse.

✓ **Make a Plan to Leave**: If you decide to leave the relationship, it is important to make a plan to do so safely. This can include contacting a shelter or safe house, securing transportation, and notifying law enforcement.

For example, you can contact a domestic violence shelter to make arrangements to stay there temporarily. You can also notify the police and request an escort to safely leave your home.

✓ **Use Technology Safely**: Abusers may use technology to monitor and control their partners. Be aware of the ways in which your abuser may be using technology to track your movements, monitor your communication, or control your finances.

For example, you can use a private browser or clear your search history to prevent your abuser from tracking your online activity. You can also disable location services on your phone or use a secondary phone that your abuser does not know about.

✓ **Trust Your Instincts**: If you feel unsafe or in danger, trust your instincts and take steps to protect yourself. This may include leaving the situation or contacting law enforcement.

For example, if your abuser becomes violent, trust your instincts and try to get to a safe place. You can also call the police or a domestic violence hotline for immediate assistance.

Remember, you are not alone. There are resources and support available to help you stay safe and leave an abusive relationship. By developing a safety plan, seeking support, and trusting your instincts, you can take steps to protect yourself and move towards a safer and healthier future.

No One Has to Be Alone: The Vital Importance of Building a Support System

Women who experience gender-based violence often feel isolated, scared, and powerless. Developing a support system can be an essential step towards healing and recovery.

A support system refers to a network of people who can provide emotional, practical, and sometimes financial assistance to those in need. The support system can include family, friends, professionals, and community resources. Developing a solid support system is especially important for women experiencing gender-based violence.

Research shows a robust support system can enhance longevity, lower stress levels, and improve mental health. We can develop a sense of belonging by building friendships with other women, which will support us as we face difficulties in life and rejoice in their victories. Our support system can significantly impact our lives, whether it's a friend to joke with or a listening ear during a trying moment.

Increasing Your Support System

It can be intimidating to start from scratch when building a support system of pals. But you may create lasting connections with only a few straightforward steps.

- ✓ **Determine potential pals**: Consider the females in your life who are compatible with your interests and principles. These might be coworkers, neighbours, or associates from a club you participate in, like a book club or fitness class. Speak with them and offer to meet for lunch or coffee.
- ✓ **Be open and sincere**: While making new acquaintances, it's crucial to be sincere and honest about who you are and what you need. Talk about how you're feeling and listen intently to theirs. You can do this to develop intimacy and trust in your relationships.
- ✓ **Make time for one another**: Finding time to catch up with pals can be difficult with busy schedules. But setting up frequent get-togethers, once a week or once a month, can help you remain in touch and strengthen your relationship.
- ✓ **Support one another**: Giving and receiving assistance is the foundation of a support system. When your friends need

you, be there for them, and don't be embarrassed to ask for assistance. Your buddies are there for you, whether you need someone to weep on or help you with an actual project.

Taking Care of Your Support System

After you've established your support system, it's critical to maintain and strengthen your connections. The following advice can help you keep your friendships strong throughout time:

- ✓ **Regularly contact** your friends by email, SMS, or phone calls. Even if you can't meet in person, keeping in touch will help keep your relationship strong.
- ✓ **Celebrate achievements**: Take the time to recognise your friends' accomplishments, whether it be a birthday, promotion, or another milestone. This will demonstrate your concern and support for them.
- ✓ **Show your interest in their lives**: Ask your pals about their interests, pastimes, and aspirations to show that you are interested in one another's lives. This will improve your bond with them and help you get to know them better.
- ✓ **Be adaptable and forgiving:** Plans can occasionally change due to the uncertainties of life. Be understanding and forgiving when your pals have to reschedule or cancel arrangements. Remember that your friendship is more significant than any activity or event.

The Advantages of a Support System

For women, developing a network of friends can have a variety of advantages. Here are a few examples:

- ✓ **Emotional support**: In times of difficulty, your friends may offer consolation and encouragement and a secure environment to express your thoughts and feelings.
- ✓ **Practical advice**: Your friends can provide practical advice and perspective based on their own experiences when you are faced with a challenge or dilemma.
- ✓ **Social interaction**: Hanging out with pals might make you feel less alone and more like a part of the world. This may be particularly significant.

In addition to family and friends, many community resources are available to women experiencing gender-based violence. These resources can provide emotional support, counselling, legal advice, and other forms of assistance. Some of the most common resources include:

- ✓ **Domestic violence hotlines**: Domestic violence hotlines provide confidential support to those experiencing abuse. They can offer advice, referrals, and assistance with safety planning. **List of Indian and International Hotlines & Helplines is provided in the Appendix.**
- ✓ **Counselling services**: Counseling services can provide a safe and supportive environment for women to talk about their experiences and work through the trauma of gender-based violence. Counselling services may be available through community organisations, healthcare providers, or private therapists. **List of Indian and International Counselling services is provided in the Appendix.**
- ✓ **Legal assistance**: Legal assistance can be critical for women experiencing gender-based violence. Many organisations

provide free or low-cost legal services to victims of domestic violence, including help with protective orders, custody arrangements, and divorce proceedings.

- ✓ **Emergency shelters**: Emergency shelters provide safe housing for women and children fleeing abusive situations. They can provide food, clothing, counselling, and other forms of support. Eg., the One-Stop Centers in India (details provided in Chapter 7).
- ✓ **Support groups**: Support groups can be valuable for women experiencing gender-based violence. They provide a safe and supportive environment for women to connect with others who have experienced similar situations. Support groups may be available through community organisations, healthcare providers, or online.

Developing a support system can take time and effort. Still, it is essential to healing and recovery for women experiencing gender-based violence. It is essential to remember that no one deserves to experience abuse, and help is available. If you or an acquaintance is experiencing gender-based violence, contact a trusted loved one or community resource for assistance. You do not have to face this alone.

Chapter Summary:

1. A safety plan is super important for women to protect themselves from violence.
2. A safety plan consists of the identification of a safe place, the creation of a communication plan and the collection and safekeeping of important documents and items.

3. Developing a safety plan, seeking support, making a plan to leave, safe use of technology and trusting your instincts are some tips women can use to stay safe while in an abusive relationship.
4. A support system of friends, family and community resources is crucial for women suffering from gender-based violence.

CHAPTER 7

JUSTICE AND PROTECTION: LEGAL REMEDIES AND RESOURCES FOR WOMEN'S SAFETY AT HOME

Legal Rights & Support Systems

While studying at the Indian Institute of Management, Ahmedabad, Rita met Raghav, one year her senior, and began a romantic relationship with him.

However, as their relationship developed, Rita noticed that Raghav displayed abusive behaviour towards her, such as verbal insults, possessiveness, and jealousy. She was instantly reminded of the abuse she had suffered at the hands of her uncle during her childhood.

Rita tried to salvage the relationship but eventually realised it was abusive and sought legal help. With the assistance of a lawyer and support from family and friends, Rita obtained a restraining order against Raghav to prevent him from contacting or approaching her.

Despite the ordeal, Rita managed to move on with her life, excelling in her studies and work and advocating for domestic abuse awareness. ***(TO BE CONTINUED)***

Victims of domestic violence often feel trapped, helpless, and alone, with no way out of the situation. In addition, many women and girl victims of violence are unaware of the legal options available to protect them in emergencies.

Awareness of legal support is the first step towards claiming legal help for abuse victims.

However, legal options and remedies available to victims of domestic violence can provide them with protection and support. In this chapter, we will detail out the laws and legal options available to victims of domestic violence, including restraining orders and criminal charges.

Did You Know:

There are many inspiring stories of women who have taken a legal stand against gender-based violence and achieved justice and empowerment. Here are a few examples:

1. ***Bhanwari Devi:*** *In 1992, Bhanwari Devi, a social worker from Rajasthan, was gang-raped by upper-caste men when she attempted to stop a child marriage. Despite facing societal stigma and threats, she filed a case against her attackers, which ultimately led to the landmark Vishakha guidelines that provided guidelines for sexual harassment in the workplace. Bhanwari Devi's case*

sparked a nationwide conversation about violence against women and paved the way for legal reform.

2. **Mukhtar Mai:** *Mukhtar Mai, a survivor of gang rape in Pakistan, refused to be silenced by her attackers and took them to court instead. Her case gained international attention and led to the conviction of six men. She used the compensation money she received to start schools and a women's shelter in her village and has become an advocate for women's rights in Pakistan.*
3. **Waris Dirie:** *Waris Dirie is a Somali-born model, author, and activist who survived female genital mutilation (FGM) and fled her home country to escape an arranged marriage. She has eversince become a vocal advocate for the abolition of FGM. She has worked with the United Nations to raise awareness of the issue. Her activism has led to legal reforms in many countries and has helped to protect countless girls from the harmful practice of FGM.*

These women, and many others like them, have shown incredible resilience and courage upon facing gender-based violence. Their legal actions and activism have helped create a more just and safer world for women and girls.

Legal Recourse: Laws that Protect Women in India

In India, domestic violence is primarily directed towards women, who are often abused by their husbands or other male family members. To address this problem, India has enacted a series of laws to prevent and address gender-based violence at home.

WOMEN-SPECIFIC LEGISLATION IN INDIA

The Protection of Women from Domestic Violence Act, 2005

This law is a crucial legislation in India that aims to protect women from violence within the domestic sphere. Here are five detailed points about the Act:

- ☐ Scope of the Act: The Act defines domestic violence as any physical, sexual, verbal, emotional or economic abuse a woman may face in her marital or familial relationships. The Act recognises the need to protect women from the violence that occurs within the domestic sphere, including acts of cruelty, dowry harassment, and marital rape.
- ☐ Protection Measures: The Act provides for a range of protection measures for women who are victims of domestic violence, including the right to reside in the shared household, protection orders to prevent the assailant from committing any acts of violence, and monetary reliefs to compensate for any losses or injuries suffered by the victim.
- ☐ Duties of the Respondent: The Act imposes specific duties on the respondent (the person accused of committing domestic violence), including the obligation to not commit any acts of violence against the victim, to provide financial support to the victim, and not dispose of any property that may be subject to the relief claimed by the victim.
- ☐ Role of Protection Officers: The Act provides for the appointment of Protection Officers responsible for assisting the victim in filing complaints and seeking protection orders. Protection Officers may also provide the victim with

counselling and legal aid and can take steps to ensure that the court orders are enforced.

- ☐ Penalties for Violation: The Act imposes penalties on people who violate its provisions, including imprisonment and fines. The Act recognises domestic violence as a severe offence and provides strict penalties to deter individuals from committing such acts.

Example: A woman named Rekha is married to a man who is physically abusive towards her. He regularly beats her and has even threatened to kill her. Rekha can seek protection under the Protection of Women from Domestic Violence Act, 2005. She can apply for a protection order requiring her husband to stop abusing her or a residence order allowing her to live separately from him. She can also seek monetary relief to support herself and her children and custody orders to protect her children from her abusive husband.

The Sexual Harassment of Women at the Workplace (prevention, prohibition, and redressal) Act, 2013:

The Sexual Harassment of Women at the Workplace (prevention, prohibition, and redressal) Act, 2013, is an Indian legislation that aims to prevent and address sexual harassment of women in the workplace. Here are five detailed points about the Sexual Harassment of Women at Workplace Act, 2013:

- ☐ Definition of sexual harassment: Sexual harassment, as defined by the Act, is any unwelcome physical, verbal, or non-verbal act of a sexual nature that creates an intimidating or hostile work environment for women. This includes physical contact and advances, sexual remarks, showing pornographic material, or any other kind of unwelcome physical, verbal or non-verbal conduct.

- ☐ Obligation of employers: The Act imposes a duty on employers to provide a safe and secure work environment for women and to prevent sexual harassment in the workplace. Employers must set up an Internal Complaints Committee (ICC) at each office or place of work with at least one woman member and implement measures to prevent sexual harassment.
- ☐ Procedure for filing a complaint: The Act provides a procedure for filing a complaint of sexual harassment at the workplace. The complainant can file a written complaint with the ICC or the Local Complaints Committee (LCC) within three months of the incident. The ICC/LCC is required to complete the inquiry and submit its report within 90 days.
- ☐ Protection against retaliation: The Act protects the complainant against retaliation for filing a complaint of sexual harassment. The employer cannot terminate, demote, or transfer the complainant or subject her to any other discriminatory practice as a result of filing a complaint.
- ☐ Punishment for non-compliance: The Act prescribes punishment for non-compliance by the employer, including a fine, imprisonment, or both. If an employer fails to follow the provisions of the Act, he may be fined up to Rs. 50,000. Repeated non-compliance may lead to the cancellation of the employer's license or registration to conduct business.

Example: A woman named Seema works in a corporate office. Her boss has been making unwelcome sexual advances towards her and has even threatened to fire her if she doesn't comply with his demands. Seema can file a complaint under the Sexual Harassment of Women at the Workplace (prevention, prohibition, and redressal) Act, 2013. The Internal Complaints Committee would then investigate the complaint and take appropriate action against her boss, including disciplinary action or termination of employment.

The Dowry Prohibition Act, 1961

The Dowry Prohibition Act of 1961 is an Indian legislation prohibiting dowry giving or taking in marriages. Here are five detailed points about the Dowry Prohibition Act 1961:

- ☐ Definition of dowry: The Act defines dowry as any valuable security or property given or agreed to be given by one party to a marriage to the other party. Dowry can be in the form of cash, jewellery, or other gifts. It is provided with the expectation that it will provide financial security to the husband or his family.
- ☐ Prohibition of dowry: The Act prohibits the giving or taking of dowry in marriages. Anyone who gives, takes, or abets the giving or taking of dowry can be punished under the Act.
- ☐ Punishment: The Act provides strict punishment for those violating its provisions. Anyone who gives, takes, or abets the giving or taking of dowry can be punished with imprisonment for up to five years and a fine of up to Rs. 15,000. The court can also order the forfeiture of any valuable security or property given or agreed to be given as dowry.
- ☐ Presumption of guilt: The Act creates a presumption against anyone accused of giving or taking dowry. The responsibility is

on the accused party/parties to show that no dowry was given or taken.

- ☐ Reporting of offences: The Act places a duty on anyone who has information about the giving or taking of dowry to report the crime to the authorities. Failure to report an offence can result in a fine of Rs. 1,000 or imprisonment for up to six months. The Act also makes it mandatory for the police to investigate any complaint of dowry harassment or dowry death.

Example: A woman named Neha is getting married to a man named Raj. Raj's family demands a large dowry from Neha's family, including cash, jewellery, and other expensive gifts. Neha's family cannot afford to pay for the dowry. Still, Raj's family threatens to cancel the wedding if their demands are unmet. Neha's family can file a complaint under the Dowry Prohibition Act 1961. If convicted, Raj and his family can be punished with imprisonment for up to five years and a fine.

The Criminal Law (Amendment) Act, 2013

The Criminal Law (Amendment) Act, 2013, also known as the **Nirbhaya Act**, was enacted to address violence against women in India. Here are five detailed points about the Act:

- ☐ Expanded the definition of rape: The Act expanded the definition of rape to include new forms of sexual assault, such as penetration with any object and non-consensual oral sex.
- ☐ Increased punishment for rape: The penalty for rape was increased from a minimum of seven years to a minimum of 10 years. Sometimes, the maximum sentence was increased from life imprisonment to the death penalty.

- ☐ Criminalised acid attacks: The Act introduced specific provisions to criminalise acid attacks, which involve throwing acid on someone intending to cause harm. The punishment for acid attacks was increased from a minimum of three to 10 years. The maximum sentence was raised to life imprisonment.
- ☐ Criminalised stalking: The Act introduced specific provisions to criminalise stalking, which involves following or contacting someone repeatedly with the intent to cause fear or distress. The punishment for stalking was increased to a maximum of three years.
- ☐ Strengthened the law against trafficking: The Act strengthened the law against human trafficking by increasing the punishment for trafficking to a minimum of seven years and a maximum life imprisonment and by including new forms of trafficking such as forced labour and begging. The Act also introduced provisions to protect victims of trafficking, including the establishment of special courts for trafficking cases and the provision of rehabilitation and compensation for victims.

Example: A group of men are accused of gang-raping a woman on a bus. The woman's injuries are severe, and she eventually dies. The men can be charged under the Criminal Law (Amendment) Act, 2013. The Act provides for more severe punishments for sexual offences, including the death penalty in some instances. The Act also criminalises new crimes, such as acid attacks and stalking. It provides for more stringent punishments for repeat offenders.

The 2006 Prohibition of Child Marriage Act

The 2006 Prohibition of Child Marriage Act is a law enacted in India to prohibit child marriages and protect children's rights. Here are five detailed points about the Act:

- ☐ Age of marriage: The Act sets the legal age of marriage as 18 years for females and 21 years for males. Any marriage involving individuals below these ages is considered voidable.
- ☐ Punishment: The Act makes child marriage a punishable offence for all parties involved, including the parents, guardians, and the person solemnising the marriage. The punishment for the crime is imprisonment of up to two years and/or a fine of up to Rs. 1 lakh.
- ☐ Protection of children: The Act recognises the right of every child to a safe and healthy childhood and seeks to protect children from the harmful effects of child marriage, including early pregnancy and childbirth, maternal mortality, and social and economic disempowerment.
- ☐ Child marriage prevention officers: The Act provides for the appointment of Child Marriage Prevention Officers (CMPOs) in every district to prevent child marriages and protect children from the harmful effects of such marriages. The CMPOs can issue injunctions against child marriages, rescue and rehabilitate child brides, and initiate legal action against offenders.
- ☐ Support for victims: The Act recognises the need for support and rehabilitation of child brides and provides for the establishment of welfare boards to provide assistance and support to victims of child marriage, including medical and psychological care, education, and vocational training. The Act also has provision

for the appointment of Child Marriage Prohibition and Protection Officers to oversee the implementation of the Act at the local level.

Example: Rukmini Kumari, a 16-year-old girl from Rajasthan, was set to be married off by her parents. Thanks to the intervention of the local authorities, the wedding was stopped, and her parents were charged under the Act for promoting child marriage. Rukmini was provided with counselling and support to prevent her from being forced into marriage again.

Juvenile Justice (Care and Protection of Children) Act, 2015

The Juvenile Justice (Care and Protection of Children) Act, 2015 is an Indian law that aims to provide care, protection, and rehabilitation to children in need of care and safety and to establish a separate justice system for juveniles who come into conflict with the law. Here are five detailed points about the Act:

- ☐ Age of juveniles: The Act defines a juvenile as a person who is below the age of 18 years. This age limit aligns with the United Nations Convention on the Rights of the Child, to which India is a signatory.
- ☐ Child welfare committees: The Act provides for establishing Child Welfare Committees (CWCs) in every district to ensure the care, protection, and rehabilitation of children in need of care and security. The CWCs have the power to make decisions regarding the care and safety of children, including their placement in institutions, and to initiate legal action in cases of child abuse, neglect, or exploitation.

- ☐ Juvenile justice boards: The Act establishes Juvenile Justice Boards (JJBs) in every district to deal with cases of juveniles who conflict with the law. The JJBs can inquire into alleged offences committed by children and pass orders for their care, protection, treatment, or rehabilitation. The Act also establishes observation homes for the temporary reception and care of juveniles who conflict with the law.
- ☐ Rehabilitation and social reintegration: The Act emphasises the importance of rehabilitation and social reintegration of juveniles who conflict with the law. It provides a range of measures to ensure juveniles' physical, emotional, and psychological well-being, including counselling, vocational training, and education.
- ☐ Protection of rights: The Act recognises children's rights, including education, health, nutrition, and safety from abuse, neglect, and exploitation. It also provides for the appointment of child advocates to protect and promote the rights of children needing care and protection and the rights of juveniles who come who break the law.

Example: Meena, a 14-year-old girl, was physically abused by her father. Meena's mother filed a complaint with the authorities. Meena was removed from the home and placed in a childcare institution under the Act. Meena was provided with counselling and support to recover from the abuse. Her father was charged and tried under the Act for committing an offence against a child.

Immoral Traffic (Prevention) Act, 1956

Trafficking by close relatives, such as parents, siblings, or other family members, is a severe form of exploitation and violence against women and children. This form of domestic trafficking includes recruiting, transporting, transferring, harbouring, or receiving persons through force, coercion, deception, or other forms of exploitation by a family member. Victims of domestic trafficking may be subjected to forced labour, sexual exploitation, or forced marriage, among other forms of exploitation. Children may be sold or given away by their parents or other family members for exploitation. The impact of domestic trafficking can be severe, especially on children, who may experience physical and emotional abuse, loss of education, and long-term psychological trauma.

The Immoral Traffic (Prevention) Act 1956 is an Indian law aimed at preventing the trafficking of women and children for prostitution and providing for the rehabilitation of victims. Here are five detailed points about the Act and its relevance for women's safety at home:

- ☐ Prohibition of trafficking: The Act makes it illegal to traffic women and children for prostitution or to buy or sell sex. This provision helps to protect women and children from being lured or coerced into prostitution, which is often a form of exploitation and violence against women.
- ☐ Punishment for offenders: The Act provides strict punishment for those who engage in trafficking or prostitution. This includes imprisonment, fines, and forfeiture of property. This

serves as a deterrent for those who may consider engaging in such activities and helps to protect women from exploitation.

- ☐ Protection for victims: The Act provides for rehabilitating victims of trafficking and prostitution. This includes medical, legal, and social assistance, vocational training and education. This helps to protect women who may have been forced into prostitution from further exploitation and to ensure their safe reintegration into society.
- ☐ Special courts: The Act provides for establishing special courts to deal with cases related to trafficking and prostitution. These courts are designed to ensure speedy and efficient justice for victims and to provide a safe and supportive environment for them to testify.
- ☐ Prevention and awareness: The Act emphasises the importance of prevention and awareness-raising activities to combat trafficking and prostitution. It calls for the involvement of government agencies, NGOs, and civil society in implementing prevention strategies, such as education and awareness-raising campaigns. This helps to prevent women from falling prey to trafficking and prostitution and promotes their safety and well-being at home.

Example: Geeta was trafficked by her own husband for prostitution. She was rescued by the police during a raid, and her husband was arrested and charged under the Act for promoting and facilitating prostitution. Geeta was provided with counselling and support to help her recover from the trauma of being trafficked.

Pre-Conception and Pre-Natal Diagnostic Techniques (Prohibition of Sex Selection) Act, 1994

The Pre-Conception and Pre-Natal Diagnostic Techniques (Prohibition of Sex Selection) Act, 1994 is an Indian law that aims to prohibit the use of pre-conception and pre-natal diagnostic techniques for sex selection and to regulate their use for the prevention of genetic and other disorders. Here are five detailed points about the Act:

- ☐ <u>Prohibition of sex selection</u>: The Act makes it illegal to use any pre-conception or pre-natal diagnostic technique to determine the sex of the foetus. This provision helps to prevent sex-selective abortions, which are a significant contributor to the skewed sex ratio in India.
- ☐ <u>Regulation of diagnostic techniques</u>: The Act regulates pre-conception and pre-natal diagnostic techniques for medical purposes, such as detecting genetic disorders. It requires that these techniques be performed only by registered medical practitioners and diagnostic centres and only with the written consent of the pregnant woman.
- ☐ <u>Punishment for offenders</u>: The Act provides strict punishment for those violating its provisions. This includes imprisonment, fines, and suspension or cancellation of registration for medical practitioners and diagnostic centres. This serves as a deterrent for those considering sex selection and helps protect the girl child's rights.
- ☐ <u>Empowerment of women</u>: The Act aims to empower women by promoting the value of the girl child and encouraging them to take responsibility for their reproductive health. It requires

that all ultrasound machines be registered. It prohibits the use of portable ultrasound machines to prevent unauthorised sex determination. This helps to prevent discrimination against girls and promotes their equal rights.

- Prevention and awareness: The Act emphasises the importance of prevention and awareness-raising activities to combat sex selection. It calls for the involvement of government agencies, NGOs, and civil society in implementing prevention strategies, such as education and awareness-raising campaigns. This helps to prevent sex-selective abortions and promotes well-being and the safety of women and girls.

Example: Seema Devi from Haryana, who was expecting her second child. Her husband and in-laws were pressuring her to undergo a sex determination test and abort the foetus if it was female. Seema resisted and informed the authorities, who conducted a raid on the diagnostic centre where the trial was to be undertaken. The centre was sealed, and the family was charged under the Act for attempting to engage in sex selection.

WOMEN-RELATED LEGISLATION IN INDIA:

The Indian Penal Code, 1860

The Indian Penal Code 1860 is the principal criminal code of India, and it applies equally to men and women. However, the code contains specific provisions that address crimes against women and provide for their protection. Here are five detailed points about the Indian Penal Code 1860 for women:

- Crimes against women: The Indian Penal Code recognises various crimes against women, including rape, sexual harassment, dowry death, and domestic violence. These offences carry severe punishments, including imprisonment and fines, and are treated as serious crimes.

- Protection of women: The Indian Penal Code contains provisions that protect women from exploitation and abuse. For example, it criminalises the trafficking of women and girls. It prohibits force, coercion, or deceit from compelling women into marriage.
- Women as victims and witnesses: The Indian Penal Code recognises that women can be victims and witnesses in criminal cases. It contains provisions that protect women from intimidation or harassment when they come forward to report a crime or testify in court.
- Women in the criminal justice system: The Indian Penal Code recognises that women may face unique challenges in the criminal justice system. It provides for the appointment of female police officers and the establishment of women's police stations to ensure the fair and respectful treatment of women during the investigation and prosecution of crimes.
- Amendments: Over the years, the Indian Penal Code has undergone several amendments to address women's changing needs and concerns. These amendments have included the addition of new offences, such as acid attacks and voyeurism, and strengthening existing provisions to protect women from violence and abuse.

Example: A man named Rakesh is accused of raping a woman. He can be charged under Section 376 of the Indian Penal Code, 1860, which criminalises rape. If convicted, Rakesh can be imprisoned for a term of not less than seven years, which may extend to life imprisonment and a fine.

Indian Evidence Act, 1872

The Indian Evidence Act of 1872 is a legislation that governs the admissibility, relevancy, and weight of evidence in legal proceedings in India. Here are five detailed points about the Act and its relevance to women:

- ☐ Protection of victims in sexual offences: The Indian Evidence Act 1872 has specific provisions that protect the identity of victims in sexual crimes. Section 228-A prohibits the disclosure of the victim's identity, including her name, address, or any other details that may reveal her identity.
- ☐ Admissibility of electronic evidence: The Act recognises electronic evidence, such as emails, text messages, and videos, as admissible evidence in legal proceedings. This is particularly relevant for women with digital evidence of harassment, stalking, or other forms of abuse.
- ☐ Expert testimony: The Act provides expert testimony in legal proceedings, which can be helpful in cases involving medical evidence, such as rape cases. This allows medical professionals to offer their expert opinion on the nature and extent of injuries and can help determine the guilt or innocence of the accused.
- ☐ Presumption of the absence of consent: The Indian Evidence Act 1872 has a provision that states that in cases of sexual offences where the victim is a woman, the lack of support shall be presumed. This shifts the burden of proof on the accused to prove that there was consent.

- ☐ Testimony of women: The Act provides women's testimony in legal proceedings, including civil and criminal cases. This is a necessary provision that empowers women to participate in the justice system and ensures that their voices are heard.

Example: Sarita is physically abused by her husband or a family member. She may have evidence, such as medical reports, photographs, or witness testimony, that can be used to support her case. Under the Act, this evidence is admissible in court and can be used to prove the accused's guilt. Additionally, Sarita can provide her testimony in court, which will be given equal weight to any other witness. The Act also recognises that women may be reluctant to testify against family members and has provisions to protect the identity of witnesses in some instances. In cases of sexual offences or issues involving children, for example, the essence of witnesses can be saved to ensure their safety.

OTHER LEGISLATIONS OF RELEVANCE TO WOMEN:

Maintenance and Welfare of Parents and Senior Citizens Act, 2007

The Maintenance and Welfare of Parents and Senior Citizens Act, 2007 provides several key provisions that are specifically relevant to senior citizen women. Here are five key points that senior citizen women should be aware of:

- ☐ Maintenance: Under the Act, a senior citizen woman can claim maintenance from her children or relatives if they are unable to maintain themselves from their own income. This includes basic amenities like food, clothing, shelter, medical treatment, and any other necessary needs.

- ☐ Protection from abuse: The Act also provides for the protection of senior citizen women from abuse, including physical, emotional, and financial abuse. Any person who abuses a senior citizen can be punished with imprisonment for up to six months and a fine.
- ☐ Establishment of old age homes: The Act provides for the establishment of old age homes, which can provide shelter and support for senior citizen women who are unable to maintain themselves.
- ☐ Establishment of medical facilities: The Act also provides for the establishment of medical facilities, which can provide medical treatment and care for senior citizen women who require it.
- ☐ Special provisions for widows: The Act recognises that widows may be particularly vulnerable and provides for special provisions for their welfare. These provisions include the establishment of special old age homes and medical facilities for widows, as well as the provision of counseling and other support services.
- ☐ Important point to consider: Even though the Senior Citizens Act does not have provisions for removing or evicting family members from a senior citizen's property, Indian courts, including the highest court of the country, the Supreme Court of India, have allowed such removal if the family members have been harassing or not providing maintenance to the senior citizen. In situations where children have been harassing their parents to transfer property to them, courts have ordered the children's removal from the parents' home. Additionally, courts have supported the eviction of a child from the property

if the child has obtained property transfer agreements using fraudulent means to harass their elderly parent.

In conclusion, India has enacted a series of laws to prevent and address gender-based violence at home. These laws provide a wide range of remedies for victims of violence, including protection orders, monetary relief, and criminal penalties for perpetrators. However, implementing these laws has been challenging, and many women still face violence and abuse in their homes. To effectively address gender-based violence, it is crucial to not only have strong laws but also to ensure that laws are effectively enforced and that survivors have access to support services and justice.

Legal Route for Domestic Violence in India: An Overview of Options and Remedies

Domestic violence is a pervasive problem in India. In this chapter, we will understand the legal options and remedies available to victims of domestic violence in India, including restraining orders and criminal charges, with examples.

The protection of women by the domestic violence Act of 2005 (PWDVA) is a landmark legislation that aims to protect women who are domestic violence victims. The Act broadly defines domestic violence as physical, sexual, verbal, emotional, and economic abuse. Under the PWDVA, a victim can seek a protection order, a residence order, a monetary order, and a custody order.

<u>Protection Order</u>: A magistrate issues a protection order to protect the victim from any violence, threats, or harassment by

the perpetrator. The order can also prohibit the perpetrator from entering the victim's place of work or any other area frequented by the victim. A protection order can be issued even if no criminal case has been filed.

Example: Ritu is a victim of domestic violence. She seeks a protection order against her husband, who has been physically assaulting her. The Magistrate issues a protection order that prohibits Ritu's husband from entering her workplace and any other place frequented by her.

<u>Residence Order</u>**:** A residence order is issued by a Magistrate that allows the victim to stay in the shared household, even if she has no legal rights over the property. The perpetrator can be ordered to provide alternative accommodation for himself.

Example: Sunita is a victim of domestic violence. She seeks a residence order under the PWDVA, fearing being homeless if she leaves her husband's house. The Magistrate issues a residence order that allows Sunita to stay in the shared household and orders her husband to provide alternative accommodation for himself.

<u>Monetary Order</u>: A monetary order is issued by a Magistrate that directs the perpetrator to pay monetary relief to the victim. The relief can include compensation for medical expenses, loss of earnings, and other losses from domestic violence.

Example: Meena is a victim of domestic violence. She seeks a monetary order under the PWDVA, as she has suffered losses due to the violence inflicted upon her by her husband. The Magistrate issues a monetary order that directs Meena's husband to pay compensation for her medical expenses and loss of earnings.

Custody Order: A custody order is issued by a Magistrate that grants custody of the child to the victim. The perpetrator can be ordered to pay maintenance for the child.

Example: Preeti is a victim of domestic violence. She seeks a custody order under the PWDVA, fearing for her child's safety in her husband's custody. The Magistrate issues a custody order that grants control of the child to Preeti and orders her husband to pay maintenance for the child.

Criminal Charges:

Apart from seeking remedies under the PWDVA, a victim of domestic violence can also file criminal charges against the perpetrator. The relevant provisions under the Indian Penal Code (IPC) include Section 498A (Cruelty by husband or his relatives), Section 304B (Dowry death), and Section 354 (Assault or criminal force upon a woman with an intent to outrage her modesty).

Section 498A: This section deals with the offence of cruelty by husband or his relatives towards a woman. Cruelty can be physical or mental, including harassment, torture, and other forms of abuse. The punishment for this crime can range from imprisonment for up to three years as well as a fine.

Example: Smita files a complaint under Section 498A of the IPC against her husband and in-laws, alleging that they have been subjecting her to mental and physical cruelty. The police investigate the matter, and based on the evidence, they file a charge sheet against the accused. The trial court convicts the accused and sentences them to imprisonment.

Section 304B: This section deals with the offence of dowry death. Suppose a woman dies within seven years of her marriage. It is shown that she was subjected to harassment or cruelty by her husband or his relatives in connection with a demand for a dowry. In that case, it is deemed to be a dowry death. The punishment for this crime is imprisonment for a minimum of seven years and a fine.

Example: Rashi dies under mysterious circumstances, and her parents suspect that she was killed by her husband and in-laws for dowry. They file a complaint with the police, who investigate the matter and find evidence that supports the parents' allegations. The police file a charge sheet against the accused, and the trial court convicts them of dowry death.

Section 354: This section deals with the offence of assault or criminal force to a woman intending to outrage her modesty. This offence can include touching a woman's body without her consent, making sexually explicit remarks, and other forms of sexual harassment. The punishment for this offence varies from imprisonment for up to two years and a fine.

Example: Neha walks home from work when a man starts following her and making sexually explicit remarks. She tries to ignore him, but he grabs and touches her inappropriately. Neha filed a complaint with the police, who arrested the accused and charged him under Section 354 of the IPC. The trial court convicts the accused and sentences him to imprisonment.

In India, victims of domestic violence have several legal options and remedies available to them, including seeking protection orders, residence orders, monetary orders, and custody orders under the PWDVA. Additionally, victims can file criminal charges against the perpetrators under the relevant provisions of the IPC. While the legal system can be challenging to navigate, seeking redress is crucial to ensure that victims of domestic violence can live free from abuse and fear.

Global Efforts to Protect Women: Laws on Women's Safety at Home

Women's safety at home has become a global concern, with increasing incidents of violence against women and girls being reported. In response, many countries worldwide have introduced laws to promote women's safety and protect them from sexual assault, domestic violence, and many other forms of abuse. This chapter provides an overview of 24 examples of such laws from different countries worldwide.

1. **The Violence Against Women Act (VAWA), 1994 (United States):** The Violence Against Women Act (VAWA) is a US federal law that provides funding for programs aimed at preventing domestic violence, sexual assault, and stalking. The law includes provisions for protecting immigrant women and women from indigenous communities. It also contains provisions for prosecuting perpetrators of these crimes.
2. **The Domestic Abuse Bill of 2019 (United Kingdom):** The Domestic Abuse Bill in the United Kingdom creates a

legal definition of domestic abuse and prohibits perpetrators from cross-examining their victims in court. The bill also introduces new protection orders to safeguard victims of domestic abuse.

3. **The Family Homes on Reserves and Matrimonial Interests or Rights Act (FMHRIA) of 2014 (Canada):** The Family Homes on Reserves and Matrimonial Interests or Rights Act (FMHRIA) in Canada aims to protect women's property rights on First Nations reserves in domestic violence or separation cases. The law also provisions the establishment of shelters for women who are victims of domestic violence.
4. **The National Plan to Reduce Violence against Women and their Children of 2010 (Australia):** This Plan includes a range of measures such as funding for support services, public education campaigns, and research on the causes and effects of violence against women. The plan also includes provisions for protecting victims of domestic violence and prosecuting perpetrators of these crimes.
5. **The Domestic Violence Act of 1998 (South Africa):** The Domestic Violence Act in South Africa provides for the issuing of protection orders and the establishment of shelters for women who are victims of domestic violence. The law also includes provisions for counselling and victim compensation.
6. **The Prevention of Domestic Violence Act of 2007 (Thailand):** The Prevention of Domestic Violence Act in Thailand aims to prevent and protect against domestic violence and includes measures such as protection orders, counselling, and victim compensation.

7. **The Family Violence Prevention Act of 2018 (New Zealand):** The Family Violence Prevention Act in New Zealand provides protection orders, counselling, and support services for victims of family violence. The law also includes provisions for prosecuting perpetrators of these crimes.
8. **The Domestic Violence and Family Protection Act of 2009 (Fiji):** The Domestic Violence and Family Protection Act in Fiji protects victims of domestic violence and includes measures such as restraining orders and counselling.
9. **The Domestic Violence Act of 2009 (Nepal):** The Domestic Violence Act in Nepal protects women from domestic violence and includes provisions for restraining orders, counselling, and compensation.
10. **The Law on Protection of Victims of Domestic Violence of 2003 (Kyrgyzstan):** The Law on Protection of Victims of Domestic Violence in Kyrgyzstan protects victims of domestic violence and includes measures such as restraining orders, counselling, and compensation.
11. **The Law on the Prevention of Domestic Violence and Protection ofVictims of 2006 (Albania):** This Albanian law aims to prevent and protect against domestic violence and includes measures such as restraining orders, counselling, and victim compensation.
12. **The Family Law Act of 1996 (Australia):** This Act provides legal protection to women who are experiencing domestic violence. It allows an apprehended domestic violence order (ADVO) to be issued against a perpetrator, prohibiting them from contacting the victim. It can also include provisions

such as an exclusion order, which prevents the perpetrator from entering the victim's home. It was amended in 2012 to better address family violence and ensure the safety of women and children. The amendments allow for the consideration of family violence in court proceedings and require the court to prioritise the victim's safety and their children above all other considerations. The law also provides greater access to support services for victims of family violence.

13. **The Domestic Violence Act of 2007 (Kenya)**: This Act criminalises domestic violence and provides a legal framework for victims to seek protection. It allows for the issuance of protection orders, which can include provisions such as restraining orders and establishes a national council to oversee the implementation of the Act.
14. **The Domestic Violence Act of 2005 (South Africa):** This Act defines domestic violence as any form of physical, sexual, emotional or psychological abuse against women and provides for the issuance of protection orders against perpetrators. It also establishes a national council to promote and monitor the implementation of the Act.
15. **The Domestic Violence (Prevention and Protection) Act of 2010 (Bangladesh):** This Act criminalises domestic violence and provides for the issuance of protection orders, including restraining orders and eviction orders, against perpetrators. It also establishes a national council to oversee the implementation of the Act.
16. **The Domestic Violence and Victim Support Unit (DVVSU) (Ghana):** This is not a law but rather a unit within the Ghana Police Service that is dedicated to

responding to domestic violence cases. The unit provides victims counselling and support services and investigates and prosecutes perpetrators.

17. **The Women's Charter of 1961 (Singapore):** This Act was Singapore's first significant legislative effort to promote gender equality and protect women's rights. It includes provisions related to marriage and divorce, property rights, and the right to education and employment.
18. **The Domestic Violence Act of 2006 (Jamaica):** This Act criminalises domestic violence and provides for the issuance of protection orders, including restraining orders and occupation orders, against perpetrators. It also establishes a national council to promote and monitor the implementation of the Act.
19. **The Family Violence Act of 2018 (New Zealand):** This Act defines family violence as any form of physical, sexual, psychological or economic abuse against family members and provides for the issuance of protection orders against perpetrators. It also establishes a national strategy to prevent and respond to family violence.
20. **The Domestic Violence Act of 2018 (Tanzania):** This Act criminalises domestic violence and provides for the issuance of protection orders, including restraining orders and eviction orders, against perpetrators. It also establishes a national council to oversee the implementation of the Act.
21. **The Protection Against Domestic Violence Act of 2015 (Zambia)**: This Act criminalises domestic violence and provides for the issuance of protection orders, including restraining orders and eviction orders, against perpetrators.

It also establishes a national council to oversee the implementation of the Act.

22. **The Law on Comprehensive Protection Measures against Gender Violence of 2004 (Spain)**: This Law was enacted in 2004 to prevent and combat gender-based violence. The law recognises gender violence as violating fundamental human rights and establishes protective measures for victims, such as restraining orders, police protection, and shelters.
23. **The Domestic Violence Intervention Act of 2010 (Canada):** This Act was enforced to provide more excellent protection to victims of domestic violence. The law enables police to remove the perpetrator from home for up to 72 hours and allows for the issuance of restraining orders to protect the victim.
24. **The Act on Restraining Orders of 2018 (Sweden):** This Act allows victims of domestic violence to obtain a restraining order against their perpetrator, which can be enforced by the police. The Act on Support and Protection for Victims of Crime gives victims the right to access support and assistance from the government, including counselling, medical care, and financial compensation. In addition, Sweden has established a national strategy to prevent and combat violence against women, which includes measures to improve the police and judicial response to domestic violence, increase public awareness, and promote gender equality.

These are just a few of the many laws and policies implemented worldwide to promote women's safety and well-being in the home. While much work remains, these efforts demonstrate a growing recognition of the need to address domestic violence and other gender-based violence as a global human rights issue.

Empowering Indian Women through Mission Shakti and its Sub-Scheme 'Sambal'

Mission Shakti is a flagship program of the Indian government aimed at empowering women and promoting their safety and security. The program was launched in March 2020 to provide a comprehensive approach to addressing women's safety, education, and healthcare issues.

One of the key initiatives under Mission Shakti is the "Sambal" subscheme. The Sambal scheme aims to provide financial assistance to women who have been victims of domestic violence, sexual assault, or other abuse. The scheme offers a one-time grant of Rs. 20,000 to women needing financial support to start a new life or to meet their immediate needs.

To apply for the Sambal scheme: Women can visit the nearest OSC and submit an application with the necessary documents, such as proof of identity, address, and evidence of the abuse suffered. The application is then processed, and if approved, the grant is provided to the needy woman.

- ✓ The Sambal scheme is a part of the "**One Stop Centre" (OSC)** initiative, which is aimed at providing integrated support and assistance to women affected by violence. OSCs are established in every district across the country and provide a range of services, including medical assistance, legal aid, counseling, and rehabilitation support.

Scan the QR code to find the One Stop Centre closest to You:

✓ Under the Sambal scheme, women who have suffered abuse can call the One Stop Centre (OSC) helpline number 181, available 24/7, to seek assistance and support. The OSC helpline number can be accessed by women in any part of the country and is toll-free. Women can call the helpline to report incidents of abuse, seek information on available services, and receive guidance on accessing the Sambal scheme. The helpline is a crucial component of the Sambal scheme. It provides women with a reliable and accessible avenue for seeking support and assistance.

In addition to the OSC helpline, there are several other helplines in India that women can access to seek support and assistance. A comprehensive list of such helplines in India and abroad are there in the Appendix.

✓ **Beti Bachao Beti Padhao (BBBP)** is a government initiative launched in India in 2015 to address the declining female child sex ratio and promote the education and empowerment of girls. The initiative was established to reverse the trend of gender-based discrimination and create an environment where girls are valued and given equal opportunities.

The BBBP initiative focuses on three main objectives:

- Preventing gender-biased sex selection and female feticide;

- Promoting girls' education, and
- Creating an enabling environment for girls to grow and develop.

The BBBP initiative has implemented various strategies and interventions to achieve these objectives, including **awareness campaigns, advocacy, community mobilisation, and capacity building**.

The initiative also provides financial assistance to families who have given birth to a girl child and encourages adopting gender-sensitive practices and policies at all levels.

The BBBP initiative has been implemented across all states and union territories in India and has received widespread support from various stakeholders, including civil society organisations, the media, and the public.

The Beti Bachao Beti Padhao (BBBP) program can be accessed through various means in India.

1. *Online portal*: The program's official website provides information on the initiative and its various components. The website can be accessed at https://betibachaobetipadhao.co.in/.
2. *Government offices*: The program is implemented by various government departments, such as the Ministry of Women and Child Development, the Department of Education, and the Department of Health. These offices can provide information on the program and its benefits.

3. *Anganwadi Centers*: Anganwadi centres are the primary centres for delivering BBBP services. These centres provide information on the program, its benefits, and how to access them.
4. *Public campaigns*: The government conducts public campaigns to raise awareness about the program and its objectives. These campaigns are usually performed through media channels such as television, radio, and social media.
5. *Toll-free helpline*: A toll-free helpline number (1800-111-777) is available for women and girls to report any incidents of gender discrimination or to seek help and support. This helpline can also provide information on the BBBP program and how to access its services.

✓ The **Nari Adalat** is a new component designed under Mission Shakti to provide women with an alternative grievance redressal mechanism to resolve minor cases such as harassment, suppression, and deprivation of rights or entitlements. This initiative will be implemented in a phased manner and involve the formation of Nari Adalats, or women's collectives made up of dedicated and respected women who will work towards this objective. This platform will also be used to create awareness among the public and receive feedback for the improvement of schemes and for better delivery of services. The Gram Panchayats will provide logistical support for this initiative in coordination with the Ministry of Panchayati Raj, the Ministry of Rural Development, and Common Service Centres operated by the Ministry of Electronics and Information Technology.

The Sambal scheme is a significant step by the Indian Government towards providing financial support and assistance to women affected by violence. It provides a one-time grant to help them meet their immediate needs and helps them in their efforts towards rehabilitation and starting a new life. The scheme is part of a more significant effort by the Indian government to promote women's safety, security, and empowerment. It is an essential component of the Mission Shakti initiative.

Chapter Summary:

1. Legal awareness is the first step towards seeking protection.
2. Several women-specific and women-related laws exist in India to protect women at home and outside.
3. The Protection of Women from Domestic Violence Act, 2005 (PWDVA) provides many legal options and remedies to victims of domestic violence in India.
4. Many countries worldwide have laws protecting women against gender-based violence.
5. Through Mission Shakti and its subscheme "Sambal", the Government of India has started many initiatives to secure and protect women.

CHAPTER 8

OVERCOMING THE PAST: MOVING FORWARD AFTER DOMESTIC VIOLENCE

Healing the Past

Rita's father standing up to the abuse

Rita's father worked as an Engineer in Mumbai and his work kept him away from home for long durations of time.

When her father came home to spend Diwali with them that year, he walked into the home during a time when Rita's uncle was mercilessly beating her. He was completely taken aback. He promptly called the police and got his younger brother arrested.

Rita's grandparents created a ruckus. Diwali was not celebrated in that house that year. He decided to shift his wife and two children alongwith himself to Mumbai.

Around two months later, Rita, her mother and brother shifted to Mumbai with her father.

Rita's trauma manifested in the form of her waking up screaming at night. She had started having nightmares ever since her trauma began but her mother had been powerless to handle it.

Her father took her to the doctor who recommended psychotherapy for Rita. It took Rita more than a year to get over and feel safe again after the trauma. **(To be continued)**

Coping with trauma and rebuilding after domestic violence can be difficult for many women. The long term effects of domestic violence can be devastating, leaving women feeling scared, isolated, and hopeless.

However, overcoming the trauma of domestic violence and rebuilding a life free from abuse is possible.

This chapter will explore the various forms of domestic violence and their impact on a woman's life. We will also examine domestic violence's psychological and emotional effects, including trauma, anxiety, and depression.

Next, we will discuss coping strategies for women who have experienced domestic violence, such as seeking therapy, building a support network, and engaging in self-care practices. We will also provide information on safety planning, including steps women can take to protect themselves and their children.

We understand that coping with trauma and rebuilding after domestic violence is a challenging and deeply personal journey. This chapter is intended to provide women with the support, guidance, and encouragement they need to take the first steps towards healing and rebuilding their lives.

Here are five success stories of individuals who overcame trauma from domestic violence:

1. **Halle Berry**: Academy Award-winning actress Halle Berry is a domestic violence survivor who has spoken openly about her experiences. Berry was in an abusive relationship with a former boyfriend and has since become an advocate for victims of domestic violence. She has supported organisations that provide resources and shelter for survivors.
2. **Kelly Sundberg**: Kelly Sundberg is a writer and domestic violence survivor who has used her experiences to help others. In her memoir, "Goodbye, Sweet Girl," Sundberg shares her journey of leaving an abusive relationship and rebuilding her life. She has become an advocate for survivors of domestic violence and is a frequent speaker.
3. **Tarana Burke**: Tarana Burke is a survivor of sexual abuse and harassment who founded the #MeToo movement in 2006. The movement gained widespread attention in 2017, sparking a public conversation about sexual harassment and assault. Burke has since become a leading advocate for survivors of sexual violence, working to provide resources and support to those who have experienced trauma.
4. **Kavita Krishnan**: Kavita Krishnan is a feminist activist in India who has worked to raise awareness about domestic violence and sexual assault. She has organised protests and campaigns to demand justice for survivors. She has been instrumental in changing laws and policies related to violence against women in India.

5. **Christy Martin**: Former world champion boxer Christy Martin was in an abusive marriage with her former husband. Martin left the relationship and rebuilt her life, eventually returning to the boxing ring and becoming a commentator for boxing matches. She has also become an advocate for domestic violence survivors. She has used her platform to raise awareness about the issue.

The Hidden Scars: Unseen Consequences of Domestic Violence

The Psychological and Emotional Effects of Domestic Violence on Victims

Victims of domestic violence may experience a range of psychological and emotional effects, including **depression, anxiety, post-traumatic stress disorder (PTSD), and low self-esteem**. These effects can be long-lasting and may persist even after the violence has ended.

For example, victims of domestic violence may experience symptoms of PTSD, such as flashbacks, nightmares, and avoidance behaviours. They may also struggle with debilitating feelings of guilt, shame, and self-blame for the abuse they have experienced. Additionally, victims may have difficulty trusting others and forming intimate relationships due to their experiences of abuse.

The Psychological and Emotional Effects of Domestic Violence on Children

Children who witness domestic violence can also experience psychological and emotional effects. These effects can include **anxiety, depression, aggression, and difficulty in school**.

For example, children who witness domestic violence may experience nightmares, sleep disturbances, and difficulty concentrating in school. They may also have trouble forming healthy relationships later in life due to their experiences of violence and abuse.

The Psychological and Emotional Effects of Domestic Violence on Loved Ones

Loved ones of victims of domestic violence can also experience psychological and emotional effects. For example, family members and friends may feel **powerless and helpless to stop the violence, leading to guilt and anxiety**.

Additionally, loved ones may feel angry and resentful towards the abuser, as well as towards the victim, for staying in the relationship. They may also experience their own trauma and symptoms of PTSD as a result of their exposure to violence.

Healing from Domestic Violence

Healing from domestic violence's psychological and emotional effects can be long and challenging. However, healing and moving forward with the proper support and resources is possible.

For example, victims of domestic violence can benefit from therapy and support groups, which can provide a safe space to process their experiences and develop coping strategies. Loved ones can also benefit from therapy and support groups, which can help them process their trauma and learn how to support their loved ones in their healing journey.

Additionally, legal and financial resources may be available to help victims of domestic violence leave abusive relationships and rebuild their lives. These resources can include restraining orders, emergency housing, and financial assistance.

Domestic violence can profoundly impact victims' and their loved ones' psychological and emotional well-being. However, with the proper support and resources, it is possible to heal and move forward from the trauma of domestic violence. It is crucial to raise awareness about domestic violence and to provide support and resources to those who have experienced it.

Healing from Within: Coping Strategies for Overcoming Domestic Violence Trauma

Trauma can profoundly impact an individual's psychological and emotional well-being. Coping with trauma can be a challenging and complex process. Still, there are strategies and resources available to help individuals move forward.

Self-Care Strategies for Coping with Trauma

Self-care is an integral part of coping with trauma. Self-care strategies can help individuals manage stress, reduce anxiety, and promote well-being. Some examples of self-care strategies include:

- ☐ **Physical self-care**: engaging in regular exercise, eating a healthy diet, getting enough sleep, and practising relaxation techniques such as deep breathing or meditation.
- ☐ **Emotional self-care**: engaging in activities that bring joy and fulfilment, such as spending time with loved ones, pursuing hobbies, and engaging in creative activities.
- ☐ **Spiritual self-care**: engaging in activities that promote a sense of meaning and purpose, such as volunteering, practising mindfulness, or attending religious services.

Therapy for Coping with Trauma

Therapy can be an effective strategy for coping with trauma. Therapy can provide a supportive and safe space for individuals to process their experiences, develop coping strategies, and work through trauma's emotional and psychological effects.

Several different types of therapy may be helpful for individuals coping with trauma. These include:

- ✓ **Cognitive-behavioural therapy (CBT)**: CBT is a type of therapy that focuses on identifying and changing negative thought patterns and behaviours. CBT can help individuals develop coping strategies and address trauma-related negative emotions.
- ✓ **Eye Movement Desensitization and Reprocessing (EMDR)**: EMDR as a therapy involves the use of guided eye movements while thinking about traumatic experiences. EMDR can help individuals process traumatic memories and reduce the emotional intensity of those memories.

- ✓ **Dialectical Behavioral Therapy (DBT)**: DBT is a type of therapy that combines cognitive-behavioural therapy with mindfulness practices. DBT can help individuals develop coping strategies, improve emotional regulation, and build healthy relationships.

Support Groups for Coping with Trauma

Support groups can also be helpful for individuals coping with trauma. Support groups provide a safe and supportive space for individuals to connect with others who have experienced similar traumas, share their experiences, and receive emotional support.

Several types of support groups may be helpful for individuals coping with trauma. These include:

- ✓ **Trauma-focused support groups:** Trauma-focused support groups are specifically designed for individuals who have experienced trauma. These groups may be led by trained therapists or peer support specialists.
- ✓ **Peer-led support groups:** Peer-led support groups are led by individuals who have experienced trauma. These groups can provide a sense of community and understanding among those who have experienced similar traumas.
- ✓ **Online support groups:** Online support groups can provide an accessible and convenient way for individuals to connect with others who have experienced trauma. Online support groups can be found through social media platforms, forums, and dedicated support group websites.

Coping with trauma can be a complex and challenging process. Still, there are strategies and resources available to help individuals move forward. Self-care, therapy, and support groups can all be effective strategies for coping with trauma. It is essential to seek help and support when dealing with trauma and to remember that healing is a journey that takes patience and time.

Rebuilding and Moving Forward: Practical Tips for Recovery after Domestic Violence

If you have experienced domestic violence, it is essential to understand that it is not your fault. You deserve to be treated with love, respect, and kindness. It is also important to remember that healing from domestic violence is a process, and it can take time. Here are some tips for rebuilding and moving forward after experiencing domestic violence:

Setting Boundaries

Setting boundaries is crucial to rebuilding your life after experiencing domestic violence. Boundaries are the limits you set to protect your physical and emotional well-being. Here are some tips for setting boundaries:

- ✓ **Identify your needs:** Take some time to think about what you need to feel comfortable and safe. It could be physical space, emotional support, or financial security.
- ✓ **Communicate your needs**: Once you have identified them, communicate them clearly to the people in your life. Be firm and assertive when setting boundaries.

- ✓ **Stick to your boundaries**: It is essential to enforce them consistently. If someone violates your boundaries, be clear about the consequences.

For example, suppose your ex-partner continues to call and text you despite your request for no contact. You can block their number or seek a restraining order in that case.

Rebuilding Trust

- ✓ **Rebuild**: Rebuilding trust after experiencing domestic violence can be challenging, but it is possible. Here are some tips for rebuilding trust:
- ✓ **Be patient**: Rebuilding trust takes time. Being patient with yourself and the people in your life is essential.
- ✓ **Take small steps**: Start with small steps, such as meeting a friend for coffee or attending a support group meeting.
- ✓ **Trust your instincts**: Trust your instincts when building new relationships. If something doesn't feel right, it isn't.

For example, suppose you are hesitant to start dating again after experiencing domestic violence. In that case, you can start by going on group outings or getting to know someone slowly before committing to a relationship.

Finding Support and Resources

Finding support and resources after experiencing domestic violence is essential to healing. Here are some tips for finding support and resources:

- ✓ **Reach out to friends and family**: Talk to people you trust about what you have experienced. They can provide emotional support and help you find resources.
- ✓ **Seek professional help**: A counsellor or therapist can help you in processing your emotions and develop coping skills. They can also help you create a safety plan.
- ✓ **Find support groups**: Joining a support group can provide a sense of community and help you feel less alone.

For example, if you need help finding a therapist, you can contact your local domestic violence hotline for referrals. If you want to join a support group, you can ask your therapist or search online for groups in your area.

Rebuilding and moving forward after experiencing domestic violence can be challenging, but it is possible. Setting boundaries, rebuilding trust, and finding support and resources are essential to your healing process. Remember, healing takes time, and it is okay to ask for help. You deserve to live a life free from violence and full of love, respect, and kindness.

Breaking the Cycle: No Second Chances for Abusive Partners

Many women who have experienced violence in their relationships often question whether they should give their violent partners a second chance. This chapter will explore why women must not get violent partners a second chance, with detailed examples.

The Cycle of Violence

To understand why women must not get violent partners a second chance, it is crucial to understand the cycle of violence.

The process of violence is a pattern of behaviour often present in abusive relationships. It consists of three phases: the tension-building phase, the acute battering phase, and the honeymoon phase.

1. In the **tension-building phase**, the abuser becomes increasingly tense, irritable, and angry. The victim often feels like walking on eggshells, trying not to upset their partner.
2. In the **acute battering phase,** the abuser becomes violent and may physically, emotionally, or sexually abuse their partner.
3. In the **honeymoon phase**, the abuser apologises, promises to change, and tries to make up for their behaviour.

This cycle can repeat itself many times, and each time it does, the abuse tends to become more severe.

The Danger of Second Chances

Giving a violent partner a second chance can be extremely dangerous. Here are some reasons why:

- ⃠ **The cycle of violence continues:** As previously mentioned, the process of violence tends to repeat itself. If a woman gives her violent partner a second chance, the cycle will likely continue, and the abuse will escalate.
- ⃠ **The abuser may not change**: Abusers often apologise and promise to change after an abusive episode, but their behaviour rarely changes. In fact, apologies and promises to change are often part of the cycle of violence.
- ⃠ **The risk of homicide increases**: Research shows that the risk of homicide increases for women who leave their abusive

partners. Giving a violent partner a second chance puts the woman at an even greater risk of being killed.

Real-Life Scenarios

Here are some real-life scenarios of women who gave their violent partners a second chance and the consequences they faced:

Sarah: Sarah's partner was physically abusive, and she left him. However, after a few months, he convinced her to give him another chance. The abuse continued, and eventually, he killed her.

Maria: Maria's partner was emotionally abusive and cheated on her. She left him, but after a few weeks, he begged her to take him back. She did, and he continued to be emotionally abusive. Eventually, Maria realised he would never change and left him for good.

Aditi: Aditi's partner was physically abusive, and she left him. He begged her to take him back and promised to change. She did, but the abuse continued, and he eventually killed her.

These examples show how dangerous it can be to give a violent partner a second chance. The risk of harm, or even death, is too high.

In conclusion, women must not give violent partners a second chance. The cycle of violence tends to repeat itself, and the risk of harm, or even death, is too high. Abusers often apologise and promise to change, but their behaviour rarely changes. Women need to prioritise their safety and the safety of their children. If you or your acquaintance is in an abusive relationship, seek help immediately. Resources are available to help you leave safely and begin a life free from violence. Remember, you deserve to be treated with love, respect, and kindness.

Healing First: Why Rebound Relationships May Not Be the Answer

Recovering from an abusive relationship can be a long and challenging process. After ending an abusive relationship, some people may need to jump into a new relationship immediately. This is known as a rebound relationship, and it can be harmful. This chapter will explore why it is crucial to avoid rebound relationships after an abusive relationship, with detailed examples.

The Aftermath of Abuse

Leaving an abusive relationship can leave a person feeling vulnerable, lonely, and unsure of themselves. After being in a relationship where they were constantly put down, controlled, and even physically harmed, it is not uncommon for survivors to experience a range of emotions such as anxiety, depression, and PTSD.

What is a Rebound Relationship?

A rebound relationship is one that someone enters into soon after the end of a previous relationship. Often, the person seeks to avoid the negative emotions associated with the last relationship by quickly finding someone new.

The Dangers of a Rebound Relationship

Entering into a rebound relationship after an abusive relationship can be dangerous. Here are some reasons why:

- **You may be vulnerable**: After leaving an abusive relationship, a person may be weak and easily influenced. A new partner may exploit this vulnerability and become controlling or abusive.
- **You may not be emotionally ready**: Recovering from an abusive relationship takes time. Entering into a new relationship too soon can prevent a person from correctly processing emotions and healing.
- **You may repeat old patterns**: If a person does not take time to reflect on their past relationship, they may repeat the same patterns with their new partner.

Real-Life Scenarios

Here are some real-life scenarios of people who entered into rebound relationships after abusive relationships:

1. Reva left an abusive relationship and quickly entered into a new relationship. She found herself feeling lonely and looking for companionship. However, her new partner became controlling and emotionally abusive. Reva found herself repeating the same patterns she experienced in her previous relationship.
2. Sarah left an abusive relationship and immediately started dating a new partner. However, she constantly compared her new partner to her previous one. She could not let go of her past relationship and sabotaged her new one.

3. Suman left an abusive relationship and started dating someone new. However, she soon realised she was not emotionally ready for a new relationship. She needed time to heal and process his emotions before he was prepared to start a new relationship.

These examples show how dangerous it can be to enter into a rebound relationship after an abusive relationship. It is essential to take time to heal properly before entering into a new relationship.

Entering into a rebound relationship after an abusive relationship can be harmful. Abuse survivors need time to heal and process their emotions before entering a new relationship. It is crucial to avoid repeating old patterns and to prioritise their emotional and physical well-being. Remember, you deserve to be treated with love, respect, and kindness. Take time to heal and prioritise your well-being.

Chapter Summary:

1. Domestic violence has wide-ranging psychological and emotional effects on victims and their loved ones.
2. Depression and low-self esteem are some of the critical psychological and emotional effects of domestic violence on victims.
3. Anxiety and difficulty at school are critical psychological and emotional indicators of domestic violence in children.
4. Loved ones of victims of domestic violence may feel powerless and helpless in being unable to stop the violence.

5. Self-care, trauma therapy, and support groups for trauma support are vital components of a strategy for coping with the trauma of violence.
6. To rebuild and move forward in life, it's essential to set boundaries, rebuild trust and find support and resources.
7. Giving a second chance to an abusive partner may prove dangerous.
8. Recovering from an abusive relationship takes time, and entering a rebound relationship without healing may prove unhealthy.

CHAPTER 9

BREAKING THE SILENCE: PREVENTION AND ADVOCACY FOR DOMESTIC VIOLENCE AWARENESS AND ACTION

Empowering Women to Empower the Community

<u>Rita's story of sharing HER story:</u>

Rita was great in her studies. She cracked the IIT-JEE in the year 2010 with an all India ranking of 4. She was able to secure an admission in the IIT, Mumbai. After completing her Computer Engineering from IIT, she cleared the CAT examination. She secured admission in IIM, Ahmedabad.

While studying in such reputable institutions, she realised that she was not the only victim of abuse at home. Her best friend had experienced sexual abuse at home. It was an eye-opening experience for her.

While completing her Financial management from IIM, Ahmedabad, she began talking about the abuse she faced at home. Her storytelling style was so unique that it attracted students by droves.

In no time, everyone knew about Rita Anand at IIM, Ahmedabad. She became a formidable voice against gender based abuse of women at home first and the community later.

She became a LinkedIn influencer and shared her story far and wide. She was invited to deliver TEDx talks several times. Over the years, she became a prominent voice against gender based violence in her community.

Prevention and advocacy are critical components in the fight against domestic violence. Prevention strategies aim to address the root causes of domestic violence and prevent its occurrence in the first place. Advocacy strategies seek to provide support and resources to women who are already victims of domestic violence and help them protect themselves and rebuild their lives.

This chapter will explore prevention strategies such as education and awareness, early intervention, and promoting healthy relationships. It will also discuss advocacy strategies such as legal assistance, counselling and support groups, and housing assistance. Finally, it will provide real-life examples of how these prevention and advocacy strategies have helped women victims of domestic violence.

By providing a comprehensive understanding of prevention and advocacy strategies, this chapter aims to help women victims of domestic violence protect themselves and rebuild their lives.

It is essential to prioritise the safety and well-being of women victims of domestic violence. This chapter will provide valuable information and resources to support that goal.

Here are some examples of both Indian and international celebrities who have supported advocacy and prevention of gender-based violence:

Indian celebrities:

1. **Priyanka Chopra:** Priyanka Chopra is a Bollywood actress and UNICEF Goodwill Ambassador. She has been vocal about her support for the prevention of gender-based violence and gender equality. She has worked with many organisations to promote women's rights.
2. **Deepika Padukone**: Deepika Padukone is a Bollywood actress who has been open about her own experiences with depression and anxiety. She has also supported initiatives to prevent gender-based violence and promote mental health, including the Live Love Laugh Foundation.
3. **Farhan Akhtar**: Farhan Akhtar is a Bollywood actor, director, and producer who has been vocal about supporting women's rights and preventing gender-based violence. He has helped several campaigns and initiatives to raise awareness of the issue, including the MARD (Men Against Rape and Discrimination) campaign.

International celebrities:

1. **Emma Watson**: Emma Watson is a UN Women Goodwill Ambassador and British actress. She has been a vocal advocate

for gender equality and preventing gender-based violence. She has supported several initiatives to promote women's rights and empower violence survivors.

2. **Oprah Winfrey**: Oprah Winfrey is a philanthropist and an American media mogul who has strongly supported women's rights and the prevention of gender-based violence. She has helped many organisations working to support survivors of violence, including the Oprah Winfrey Leadership Academy for Girls.
3. **Meghan Markle**: Meghan Markle is a philanthropist and American actress who has been a vocal advocate for women's rights and the prevention of gender-based violence. She has supported several initiatives to promote gender equality and empower violence survivors, including the #MeToo movement.

Preventing Domestic Violence: Strategies and Interventions

Education and Awareness

Education and awareness are vital components in preventing domestic violence. By raising awareness about the warning signs of domestic violence, individuals can learn how to recognise abusive behaviour patterns and seek help when needed. Education can also help promote healthy relationships and give people the tools to maintain positive and respectful relationships.

Examples of education and awareness strategies include public campaigns, workshops, and training programs. These programs can target different audiences, such as young adults, parents, or healthcare and law enforcement professionals. For instance, a local nonprofit organisation might host a workshop for high school students on healthy relationships and warning signs of abuse.

Early Intervention

Early intervention is crucial in preventing domestic violence. It involves identifying and addressing problematic behaviour patterns before they escalate to violence. This can be achieved through education, counselling, and therapy.

Examples of early intervention strategies include anger management programs, couples counselling, and parenting classes. For example, a couple experiencing communication problems might seek advice to learn better ways to resolve conflicts and prevent escalating to physical violence.

Bystander Intervention

Bystander intervention is another important strategy in preventing domestic violence. It involves recognising and intervening when someone is in a potentially dangerous situation. Bystanders can be friends, family members, coworkers, or even strangers who witness abusive behaviour.

Examples of bystander intervention strategies include speaking up when someone is verbally or emotionally abusive, offering support to someone experiencing abuse, or calling the police in physical violence. For example, a coworker who suspects that a colleague is experiencing abuse might offer to listen and provide resources for support, such as a local domestic violence hotline.

Real-Life Scenarios

Here are some real-life scenarios of strategies for preventing domestic violence:

1. **Education and Awareness**: A local nonprofit organisation hosts a workshop for high school students on healthy relationships and warning signs of abuse.
2. **Early Intervention:** A couple experiencing communication problems seeks counselling to learn better ways to resolve conflicts and prevent escalating to physical violence.
3. **Bystander Intervention**: A coworker who suspects that a colleague is experiencing abuse offers to listen and provide resources for support, such as a local domestic violence hotline.

These examples demonstrate the importance of prevention strategies in addressing domestic violence. By providing education and awareness, intervening early, and engaging bystanders, individuals can help prevent abuse from occurring.

In conclusion, strategies for preventing domestic violence are essential in protecting individuals and promoting healthy relationships. Education and awareness, early intervention, and bystander intervention are effective strategies that can be used to prevent domestic violence. Individuals can actively prevent domestic violence by recognising the warning signs, intervening early, and engaging bystanders. We must continue prioritising prevention strategies and work towards creating a world in which everyone can live free from abuse.

Advocating Against Domestic Violence: Empowering Self and Others

For every woman who has experienced domestic violence, it is essential to know how to advocate for themselves and others affected by it, including speaking out and supporting organisations and initiatives to prevent it.

Speaking Out

Speaking out about domestic violence is one of the most powerful ways to advocate for oneself and others. By sharing personal experiences, raising awareness, and speaking up against abusive behaviour, individuals can help break the cycle of violence and promote positive change.

Examples of speaking out strategies include sharing personal experiences on social media or in public forums, participating in rallies or protests, and conversing with friends and family members about the issue. For instance, a survivor of domestic violence might share their story in a blog post or at a public event to help raise awareness and inspire others to speak out.

Supporting Organisations

Supporting organisations that prevent domestic violence is another critical way to advocate for oneself and others. These organisations provide vital resources and services to survivors and work to promote education, awareness, and prevention efforts.

Examples of organisations include local domestic violence shelters, advocacy groups, and national organisations such as the

National Domestic Violence Hotline. Individuals can support these organisations by donating money or volunteering their time. For example, someone might volunteer at a local shelter or participate in a fundraising walk for a domestic violence organisation.

Supporting Initiatives

Supporting initiatives that prevent domestic violence is another effective way to advocate for oneself and others. These initiatives can include policy changes, education programs, and public awareness campaigns.

Examples of initiatives include campaigns that promote healthy relationships, bystander intervention, and legislative efforts to strengthen domestic violence laws and increase funding for victim services. For instance, someone might sign a petition or contact their elected officials to support legislation improving protections for domestic violence survivors.

Real-Life Scenarios:

Here are some real-life scenarios of ways to advocate for oneself and others affected by domestic violence:

1. **Speaking Out**: A survivor of domestic violence shares their story in a blog post to help raise awareness and inspire others to speak out.
2. **Supporting Organisations**: Someone volunteers at a local domestic violence shelter and participates in a fundraising walk for a domestic violence organisation.

3. **Supporting Initiatives**: Someone signs a petition to support legislative efforts to improve protections for domestic violence survivors.

In conclusion, advocating for oneself and others affected by domestic violence is crucial in promoting positive change and ending the cycle of violence. By speaking out, supporting organisations, and supporting initiatives, individuals can help raise awareness, provide resources and services to survivors, and promote prevention efforts. We must continue prioritising advocacy efforts and work towards a world where everyone lives free from abuse.

Chapter Summary

1. Education and awareness, early intervention and bystander intervention are critical components of all domestic violence strategies.
2. Speaking out about and supporting organisations and initiatives is crucial to advocating for oneself and others affected by domestic violence.
3. Prevention begins before violence starts, through education and awareness that helps people recognise red flags, name abuse, and understand what healthy relationships look like.
4. Early intervention matters, because timely counselling, therapy, and behaviour support can stop harmful patterns from escalating into violence.
5. Bystanders are not powerless, friends, family, colleagues, and neighbours can speak up, offer support, and connect someone to help when they notice abuse.

6. Advocacy helps survivors rebuild, by speaking out, accessing legal and counselling support, and strengthening shelters and initiatives that protect women and expand their choices.

CHAPTER 10

SELF-EMPOWERMENT: A PATH TO PERSONAL GROWTH AND FULFILLMENT

Insight Timer App

Listen to Sia's "Unstoppable" on Youtube:
https://youtu.be/YaEG2aWJnZ8

<u>Rita's story of her Self-healing:</u>

Rita began to speak out about her experience, both to raise awareness about the prevalence of physical and sexual abuse and to help other survivors of abuse feel less alone. She started volunteering at a local shelter for survivors of domestic violence and physical assault, and eventually became a trained counsellor.

Through her work with survivors, Rita discovered that her experience could be a source of strength and resilience, rather than something to be ashamed of. She began to see herself as a survivor rather than a victim and found that empowering others was a powerful way to heal herself.

Today, Rita is a strong and confident woman, who uses her own experiences to help others overcome their own trauma.

One of the most significant gifts that nature has given us women is the incredible Power of Resilience. It's hard for us to give up. Nature loves us so much that it has gone ahead and given us the sixth sense – gut feeling, whatever you may call it. We can do anything if we give birth to an entirely new Human Being. Every era of human existence, from the ancient to the present, has seen a powerful woman challenging the existing status quo and setting new standards.

So, are these self-aware power women any different from You and me? Do you think that they had an easier life than us?

What do you think?

If you believe the answer to both the questions above is a **Yes**, you cannot be farther from the truth, dear Friend.

Women like Joan of Arc, Mirabai and Kalpana Chawla have faced the same familial and societal pressures as You and Me. But the one thing that made them super special was their mindset. They refused to let challenging situations pull them down. They knew what all they wanted, and they went ahead and grabbed it all.

Life throws lemons at all of us. Those ingenious enough to catch them and make lemonades out of them are the victors, the achievers.

Did You Know?

Incredible stories of Resilience:

1. **Malala Yousafzai:** Malala Yousafzai is the youngest Nobel Prize winner and Pakistan's most vocal voice vouching for women's education. At 15, the Taliban shot her in the skull for speaking out against their prohibition on girls' education. Malala is currently a student at the University of Oxford and continues campaigning for women's education in the face of hardship.
2. **Oprah Winfrey:** Oprah Winfrey is a philanthropist, talk show host, actress, and media celebrity. She was abused sexually as a young child and was born into poverty in a remote area of Mississippi. Oprah put in a lot of effort despite having a challenging upbringing to become one of the world's most successful and influential women.
3. **Serena Williams:** Serena Williams is a professional tennis player who has won 14 Grand Slam doubles championships and 23 Grand Slam singles championships. Despite encountering discrimination and prejudice throughout her career, she has never given up on her commitment to success. Serena has utilised her platform to speak out against injustice and is a prominent supporter of gender equality.
4. **J.K. Rowling:** One of the most popular book franchises in history, the Harry Potter series, is written by J.K. Rowling. Rowling was a welfare recipient and single mother before she became a best-selling author. Despite battling financial difficulties and publisher rejection, Rowling persisted and

ultimately rose to become one of the wealthiest women in the world.

5. **Maya Angelou:** Maya Angelou was a poet, memoirist, and civil rights advocate from the United States. She experienced sexual abuse as a young child and lived in poverty. Despite having a challenging childhood, Angelou became a renowned author and poet who won various accolades for her work. She also participated in civil rights activism, pushing for social justice and equality.

Can You and I develop such an incredible mindset?

We surely can.

Loving Yourself Unconditionally: The Key to Self-Acceptance and Confidence.

Remember the first time you were in trouble – at home or school. Remember the time when a parent or teacher was screaming at you? Who held you together and prevented you from crumbling? Who told you what to do next in a way you understood and could implement? (Most adults simply speak in a language that is difficult for children to understand; as a kid, half of the time, I didn't know why I was being shouted at!).

It was your own Self.

Most of us have seen a time when the world appears to gang up against us. But even then, your Self is your most significant friend. Your Self is always there with you.

But whom do we put down the most in our entire lives? It's our Self.

I am not good enough.

I always fail.

I can never succeed.

I am not pretty/ handsome enough.

Who are we hurting most when we say all this? It is our Self.

If you cannot love yourself, how can you love anyone else? This is the biggest problem plaguing most women today. As women, we are taught to put ourselves last. Sadly, many women have lost themselves under the mountainous responsibility of being the nurturers of the family.

One of the most iconic Bollywood dialogues of all time is from the movie, 'Jab We Met':

"Main Apni Favorite Hoon".

So, come on, let's love ourselves like never before. If not more than our family, then at least as much as we love our family. But we must start somewhere.

Tips to love ourselves like never before:

☐ For at least 10 minutes daily, do something that you really enjoy doing, for e.g., treating yourself to a piping hot cup of tea/ coffee, simply sitting in silence and enjoying the solitude, reading a book, going out for a walk, going to the salon, waking up early in the morning and going out and breathing in the morning air, meditation, coding – anything that you absolutely love. During this 10-minute "Me-Time", think about your current life and solutions to pressing problems presently bugging you. I use this time to think about what I want to do with my life.

☐ Learn to say "No" to things you are uncomfortable with at home and outside: As women, we are taught to be all accepting. But we must learn to draw the line and not take everything thrown our way. Saying 'No' is not a crime! One easy way to learn to say no is to start saying it in low-stakes (low pressure, fewer consequences) situations, such as saying no to attending a social event, refusing to help someone when you seriously don't have the time and energy to do it, etc. Another helpful tip to help you learn to say "No" is offering alternate solutions or compromises to situations where you want to say No. For e.g., saying, "I'm not able to do that, but I can offer this instead.", "I can't do it alone, but maybe we could work together to find a solution.", "I can't commit to that timeline, but what if we aim for a later date?" etc.

☐ Care for your mental and physical health. Eating healthily, sleeping for eight hours every night, and exercising at least five days a week are the three most straightforward ways to stay fit mentally and physically.

☐ Talk positively with yourself. Replace all the negative things we say ourselves with positive phrases and words. Instead of saying, "I am not good at doing ______", say, "I am great at doing ___________". Instead of repeatedly saying, "I am not good enough", repeatedly say, "I am awesome!" Instead of saying, "I am a loser," say, "I am unstoppable."

- ☐ Embrace your originality. Cherish your uniqueness and embrace your peculiarities and flaws to make yourself distinct. Understand that these are what make you special and unique. As a child, I was always put down for being a rebel. There was a time when I hated myself for being a rebel. But this rebellious attitude helped me stand up to sexual violence. This rebelliousness helped me find and marry my soulmate. Accept everything about you that others and you perceive as imperfections.
- ☐ Forgive yourself for past and present mistakes. Learn to let go of guilt or shame within yourself by forgiving yourself for previous and current wrongdoings. Be kind and compassionate to yourself just as you would to a friend.

Overcoming Guilt: Empowering Women to Move Beyond Shame and Self-Blame

Guilt is a powerful emotion that can impact every aspect of a woman's life. From the guilt of past trauma to the guilt of daily life choices, women face a wide range of experiences that can lead to feelings of guilt. In this chapter, we will explore some of the most common types of guilt that women may experience, including abuse related guilt, motherhood guilt, career guilt, body guilt, relationship guilt, and financial guilt.

Abuse Related Guilt:

One of the most common types of guilt that women may experience is abuse related guilt. Women who have experienced abuse may feel guilty for a variety of reasons. They may blame themselves for the abuse or feel that they somehow caused it. They may also feel guilty for not leaving the situation sooner or for not speaking up about what happened.

For example, Sarah was sexually abused by her uncle when she was a child. She spent years feeling guilty for what happened, even though she knew that it wasn't her fault. She felt like she should have been able to stop the abuse or speak up about it sooner.

Motherhood Guilt:

Many women experience guilt related to motherhood. They may feel guilty for not spending enough time with their children or for not being the "perfect" mother. They may also feel guilty for pursuing their own interests or career, which can lead to conflicting feelings about their role as a mother.

For example, Maya struggled with motherhood guilt when she returned to work after having her first child. She felt like she was missing out on important moments with her baby and worried that she wasn't being a good enough mother. At the same time, she enjoyed her work and felt fulfilled by her career.

Career Guilt:

Women may also experience guilt related to their careers. They may feel guilty for pursuing their professional goals at the expense of their personal life or for not living up to their own expectations. They may also feel guilty for not earning enough money or for not being successful enough in their career.

For example, Aisha had always dreamed of being a successful lawyer. However, when she finally achieved her goal, she found herself struggling with career guilt. She felt like she was neglecting her personal life and worried that she wasn't making a meaningful impact in the world.

Body Guilt:

Many women also experience guilt related to their bodies. They may feel guilty for not looking a certain way or for not being able to maintain a certain weight. They may also feel guilty for indulging in "unhealthy" behaviors or for not being physically active enough.

For example, Nisha struggled with body guilt after having children. She felt like her body had changed in ways that were unattractive and was often self-conscious about her appearance. She also felt guilty for not being more disciplined with her diet and exercise routine.

Relationship Guilt:

Women may also experience guilt related to their relationships. They may feel guilty for not being a good enough friend, partner, or family member. They may also feel guilty for not being able to maintain certain relationships or for not being able to meet the expectations of others.

For example, Priya struggled with relationship guilt when she ended a long-term relationship with her boyfriend. She felt like she was letting him down and worried that she wasn't being a good partner. She also felt guilty for not being able to maintain the relationship, even though she knew that it wasn't healthy for either of them.

Financial Guilt:

Finally, women may also experience guilt related to their finances. They may feel guilty for not being able to provide for their family or for not being able to manage their finances effectively. They may also feel guilty for spending money on themselves or for not contributing enough to charitable causes.

For example, Deepa struggled with financial guilt when she lost her job during the pandemic. She felt like she was letting down her family by not being able to contribute to household expenses. She also felt guilty for not being able to save enough money for emergencies or for not being able to donate as much to charity as she would like.

Some strategies that can help women overcome feelings of guilt:

- ✓ **Identify the source of guilt**: To overcome guilt, it's important to first identify the source of the guilt. This can help women better understand why they are feeling guilty and develop a plan to address the underlying issues.
- ✓ **Practice self-compassion**: Women should practice self-compassion by being kind and understanding towards themselves. They should recognise that everyone makes mistakes and that it's okay to make mistakes.
- ✓ **Challenge negative self-talk**: Negative self-talk can contribute to feelings of guilt. Women should challenge negative self-talk by replacing negative thoughts with positive affirmations.

- ✓ **Take responsibility and make amends**: If the guilt is related to a specific action or behaviour, it's important to take responsibility and make amends. This can help women feel better about themselves and move forward.
- ✓ **Seek support:** Women should seek support from friends, family, or a therapist. Talking to someone about their feelings can help them gain perspective and develop strategies for coping with guilt.
- ✓ **Practice mindfulness**: Mindfulness can help women focus on the present moment and reduce feelings of guilt related to the past or future. Techniques such as meditation or deep breathing can be helpful.
- ✓ **Set realistic expectations**: Women should set realistic expectations for themselves and avoid comparing themselves to others. This can help reduce feelings of guilt related to not living up to expectations.
- ✓ **Celebrate successes**: Women should celebrate their successes, no matter how small. This can help them feel more confident and less guilty about their achievements.

Breaking the Silence: Encouraging Women to Speak Up and Seek Help for Domestic Violence

While some abuse victims might feel at ease disclosing the abuse they are going through to their family and friends, others might not feel safe or supported enough to do so. The victims may choose not to tell their loved ones about the abuse for various reasons, including fear, shame, guilt, loneliness, a lack of support, and cultural or religious beliefs. As a result, victims could feel alone, isolated, and unsure how to get assistance.

So, what are the reasons that lead to an abuse victim not asking for help?

- **Fear**: Victims might worry that if they report the abuse to anybody, their abuser will retaliate or that no one will believe them or treat them seriously.
- **Shame**: Victims who have experienced abuse may feel embarrassed or humiliated and fear their loved ones will criticise or point the finger at them.
- **Guilt**: Victims who experience abuse may feel guilty or accountable for it, and they may worry that their loved ones will accuse them of it or be disappointed in them.
- **Seclusion**: Abusers frequently try to keep their victims apart from friends and family, which makes it challenging for victims to ask for assistance.
- **Lack of support**: Victims can believe their relatives won't be there for them or comprehend what they're going through.
- **Cultural or religious beliefs**: Reporting abuse may have a stigma in some cultures or religions, or victims may worry that doing so will embarrass their family or community.

The well-being of victims and their ability to heal from the trauma of abuse can be significantly impacted by failing to report abuse to families and friends. Here are a few ways that victims may be affected by this:

- **Isolation**: Without nobody to turn to for support or advice, victims may feel isolated and alone.
- **Increased risk of harm**: Victims are more likely to suffer physical, mental, and psychological injury if they don't report their abusers' mistreatment.

- ⃠ **Self-blame**: Victims may hold themselves accountable for the abuse and feel obligated to put an end to it.
- ⃠ **Trauma symptomology**: Including anxiety, sadness, PTSD, and substance misuse. These symptoms can usually make it difficult for victims to go about their everyday lives.
- ⃠ **Lack of validation**: If their loved ones do not recognise or believe them, victims may feel their experiences are not meaningful or valid.
- ⃠ **Difficulty in asking for help**: Finding options and requesting assistance may be challenging for victims without the encouragement and support of their loved ones.

Supporting abuse victims and convincing them to seek help can indeed be done in several ways, including:

- ✓ <u>Giving them a patient hearing & validation</u>: It's critical to pay attention to victims' experiences and to validate them. Give them your support and acknowledge the validity of their experiences.
- ✓ <u>Respect their decisions</u>: It is imperative to respect victims' decisions and not put any pressure on them to report abuse or seek assistance. Provide them resources and support but give them the freedom to decide for themselves what is best for their security and well-being.
- ✓ <u>Educate</u>: Inform victims of the many forms of abuse, the effects it may have on their lives, and the support systems that are available to them.
- ✓ <u>Connect victims to resources</u>: Connecting victims to resources includes contacting them with hotlines, support groups, and

counselling services. If you can, assist them in using these resources.

- ✓ Offer safety planning: Assist victims in developing a safety plan that will enable them to remain secure in an emergency.
- ✓ Be Patient and supportive towards them: Remember that healing from abuse requires time, so be patient and encouraging. Let victims know you are available whenever they need you, and be patient and encouraging.
- ✓ Encourage to seek professional support: Urge victims to seek professional assistance from therapists or counsellors who are qualified to assist them in recovering from the trauma of abuse.

Breaking Barriers: The Importance of Women Asking for Help

Women frequently take great satisfaction in our ability to balance various obligations and tasks. Asking for assistance can seem like a sign of weakness since we want to be perceived as strong and independent. But no one can succeed on their own. For our prosperity and well-being, we must develop the skill of knowing when to ask for assistance.

According to research, women who ask for assistance are more likely to succeed in their endeavours, feel less stress and burnout, and build healthier relationships. By asking for help from others, we can access a plethora of information, tools, and viewpoints that can support us in overcoming obstacles and realising our goals.

Overcoming the Fear of Requesting help

Despite the advantages of asking for assistance, many women battle the anxiety of appearing weak or inept. Here are some suggestions for getting over that fear:

- ✓ **Acknowledge your strengths**: Remember that asking for assistance doesn't make you less capable or strong. It's merely a means of obtaining the service you require to achieve.
- ✓ **Change your perspective**: Consider asking for assistance to demonstrate vulnerability and forge connections with others rather than as a sign of weakness.
- ✓ **Practice self-compassion**: Be compassionate to yourself when you make errors or face hardships. Understand that asking for assistance is okay and that everyone needs it occasionally.
- ✓ **Start with baby steps**: If you're not used to asking for aid, start with a tiny request and increase it over time. You'll feel more confident and less anxious as a result of this.

How to ask for help:

Once you've conquered your fear of asking for assistance, knowing how to do so is crucial. Here are a few tips:

- ✓ **Be Clear and Concise**: When requesting assistance, be precise and concise about what you require and why. This will make it clearer to others how they can best assist you.
- ✓ **Be straightforward**: Don't mince words or assume that others can read your mind. Be direct when requesting what you require.

- ✓ **Be respectful**: Respect other people's time and resources while asking for assistance. Don't presume that they will stop what they are doing to assist you.
- ✓ **Be thankful**: When someone does assist you, be sure to thank them profusely and let them know how much you value their assistance.

Creating a Support System

When you have a network of friends, family, and coworkers behind you, asking for assistance when needed can be more straightforward. Here are some pointers for creating your network of supporters:

- ✓ **Reach out to others:** Don't be scared to ask for support from others by reaching out to them. You might be shocked by how helpful folks are.
- ✓ **Listen patiently and carefully**: When someone else begs for your assistance, listen carefully and provide any support you can.
- ✓ **Cultivate relationships**: Spend time and effort cultivating relationships with other people. To meet new people, go to social events, sign up for clubs or organisations, or volunteer in your neighbourhood.
- ✓ **Giving back**: Be prepared to assist and support others when required. To ensure that you have a solid support system when you need it most, it can be helpful to develop reciprocal relationships.

The Advantages of Seeking Assistance

Women can gain a lot from learning how to ask for support. Here are a few examples:

- ✓ **Increased productivity**: Gaining the assistance you require can help you be more effective and productive in your personal and professional lives.
- ✓ **Decreased stress**: You can lower your stress levels and enhance your mental health when you stop trying to handle things independently.
- ✓ **Relationships**: You can improve your connections with others by asking for assistance.

Taking Control: The Power of Saving for Women's Future.

Right from my first salary, I have religiously saved money.

I took a bank loan to pursue my MBA (Health Management) course from IIHMR, Delhi. The loan was given by considering my mom and dad's home as collateral. This weighed on my consciousness every day of my two-year course. On the first day of the MBA placements, in the first ever placement interview, I got an offer from the National AIDS Control Organization, Ministry of Health & Family Welfare, to join as a Technical Officer (Research & Development), which I gratefully accepted (I would have been raving mad to not do so!).

During my MBA, I got a need-based-merit scholarship of Rs. 50,000, which I used to repay the loan. Right from the first salary I got from NACO, I put the entire amount into repaying the loan. In less than a year, I repaid the Rs. 4 lakh loan. My banker humorously asked me to never come back to ask them for a loan, as I had not given them much of an opportunity to make money in terms of interest amount.

This feat gave me such an incredible high that I was hooked on saving even after entirely repaying my loan amount. Before marriage, I had only transport expenses to care for, so I began saving around 90% of my salary.

Saving consistently every month for seven years gave me a substantial corpus to fund my marriage. I took limited financial assistance from my mom and dad here to not make them feel bad for being unable to contribute to their daughter's wedding. I did not burden my mom and dad and did not jeopardise their old age by making them invest their life savings into my marriage.

This corpus also helped me fund my honeymoon to Sri Lanka, support my daughter's delivery and helped me fund many courses that I did, which helped me write this book.

Women must manage their finances and make plans for the future. Saving money each month is one of the most crucial things we can do to achieve this.

The Advantages of monthly savings

The advantages of saving money each month are numerous. Here are a few examples:

✓ **Financial stability**: By setting aside money each month, you can create a financial cushion that will give you security and peace of mind. Having savings can make you feel more in control of your finances, whether you need to make up for unforeseen costs or are making retirement plans.

- ✓ **Financial long-term objectives**: Setting aside money each month can help you reach long-term financial objectives like buying a home, establishing a business, or saving for retirement. You can move closer to these objectives over time by allocating a portion of your money each month.
- ✓ **Creation of an Emergency Fund**: Saving money each month might help you create an emergency fund that you can use to pay for unforeseen needs like auto repairs or medical bills. An emergency fund can prevent you from incurring debt or using credit cards to pay these costs.
- ✓ **Peace of mind**: Reducing stress and bringing about peace of mind can be achieved by having funds. You'll have a backup plan if something unforeseen occurs, which might make you feel more assured and in charge.

How to Create Monthly Savings

Saving each month can seem complex, mainly if your finances are limited. However, there are several methods you may employ to make saving simpler and more manageable:

- ✓ **Set a savings goal**: Decide how much you want to save each month and why. You may be more inclined to save if you have a definite objective.
- ✓ **Establish a budget**: You may track your spending using a budget and find areas where you can save. You can have more money to put towards savings if you lower your spending.

- ✓ **Automate your savings**: Create monthly automated transfers from your checking account to a savings account. You can save regularly by doing this without having to think about it.
- ✓ **Develop a saving habit**: Approach saving like any other habit, like working out or eating well. Make saving a priority and commit to doing so, even if it's just a tiny amount each month.

Ways to Save More

There are various methods you can employ to increase your savings if you wish to save more money each month:

- ✓ **Spend less**: Look for areas where you may save money, such as cutting back on eating out or cancelling subscriptions to services you don't use.
- ✓ **Enhance your income**: Think about freelancing or taking on a side job. The additional funds might be used to increase your savings.
- ✓ **Take advantage of money-saving opportunities**: Keep an eye out for ways to save, such as using coupons or shopping during sales. Everything adds up in the end.
- ✓ **Prioritise your savings**: Make saving a priority by putting it at the top of your list of things to do. You'll likely follow through and save money if you prioritise it.

Where to save money every month:

Women in India have a variety of ways to save money each month, including:

- ✓ **Savings accounts**: Savings accounts are available from most Indian banks and offer attractive interest rates. It is possible to programme monthly transfers from your checking account to your savings account.

- ✓ **Fixed deposits**: Fixed deposits (FDs) are a common way to save money in India. You can receive interest by making a lump sum deposit for a predetermined time. FDs typically offer better interest rates than savings accounts.
- ✓ **Recurrent deposits (RDs)**: Just like FDs, RDs let you deposit a specific sum of money regularly for a particular time. At the end of the period, you receive the principal and interest you earned on the deposit.
- ✓ **Public Provident Fund (PPF)**: The Indian government provides PPF for long-term savings. Up to Rs. 1.5 lakh can be contributed annually, and interest on the deposit is tax-free. PPF has a 15-year minimum lock-in term.
- ✓ **National Savings Certificates (NSC)**: The Indian government provides NSC to save money. NSCs are available for a set amount of time, and you can earn interest on your deposits. Taxes must be paid on NSC interest.
- ✓ **Mutual Funds**: You can invest in a portfolio of stocks, bonds, and other securities through mutual funds. A structured investment plan (SIP), which enables you to invest a certain sum of money each month, can be used to invest in mutual funds.
- ✓ **Gold savings plans**: Several jewellers in India provide gold savings plans that allow customers to make regular payments towards the purchase of gold. You receive gold at the end of the scheme, equal to the amount you paid.
- ✓ **National Pension Scheme**: The Indian government offers a defined contribution retirement savings plan called the

National Pension Plan (NPS), which is voluntary. All Indian nationals between the ages of 18 and 65 are eligible. Individuals can routinely make contributions to their retirement savings through the NPS. Depending on the subscriber's preferences, the gifts are invested in a mixture of stock, debt, and government securities. The pension Fund Regulation and Development Authority oversees the programme (PFRDA).

In India, the National Pension Program (NPS) is a popular retirement-savings scheme that may also be helpful for women due to the following reasons:

- ✓ **Tax advantages**: Tax deductions for contributions to the NPS are allowed under Section 80C of the Income Tax Act upto a max of Rs. 1.5 lakh annually. A second tax deduction is also available for NPS payments up to Rs. 50,000 annually under Section 80CCD (1B).
- ✓ **Minimal fees**: Among Indian retirement savings programmes, the NPS has one of the lowest expense ratios[11]. The NPS levies fees based on the assets it manages, typically less than 1% annually.
- ✓ **Option for an annuity**: When you reach retirement age, you can buy an annuity using the money saved in the NPS. A financial product called an annuity offers a steady income for the rest of your life. The NPS provides a variety of annuity

[11] The expense ratio is the portion of your mutual fund investment used to cover the fund's costs, including management fees, administrative costs, and other operational costs. In other words, it's the amount that the fund charges you for managing your money. A lower expense ratio indicates that a more significant portion of your investment is used to generate returns, whereas a higher expense ratio indicates that a more substantial amount is used to cover the fund's overhead.

choices, including a combined life annuity that can financially support you and your spouse.

- ✓ **Partial Withdrawals available**: After three years of membership, you can make partial withdrawals from your NPS account in case of an emergency. Financial emergencies or unforeseen bills can benefit from this.

Taking charge of your money and making plans for the future of your finances both require regular savings. You may attain your long-term financial goals and develop financial security by defining a savings goal, making a budget, and developing a saving habit. Remember that even the smallest amount can add up, so start small and gradually increase your savings.

Unlocking Potential: How Upskilling Can be a Game Changer for Women.

In today's rapidly changing world, it has become essential for everyone to continually upskill themselves to be relevant and competitive in their various areas. But women, who historically have faced numerous obstacles to career advancement and deal with a constantly changing employment market, need upskilling even more than males.

Historical Context:

Women have faced several obstacles throughout history when it comes to getting an education and finding a job. Women were generally directed towards "traditional" female-dominated professions like teaching, nursing, or secretarial work during a significant portion of the 20th century, discouraging them from seeking higher education. As a result, they had fewer possibilities to grow in their careers. They found it more challenging to compete in industries where men predominated.

Even as women started to work in formerly male-dominated sectors, they encountered prejudice and discrimination, with many businesses choosing to recruit men or paying women less and giving them fewer prospects for promotion. Because of the legacy of prejudice and bigotry that still affects women today, it is crucial for them to continuously improve their skills to remain competitive.

The Benefits of Upskilling for women:

Women who want to succeed in their careers might benefit from upskilling in various ways. Women may boost their value to their employers and their prospects of finding new opportunities by keeping up with the most recent trends, technology, and best practices in their industry. More pay, better promotion prospects, work security, and stability are all benefits of upskilling.

In addition to these valuable advantages, upskilling can give women a sense of empowerment and confidence that can help them feel more in charge of their work lives. Women can develop the abilities and information necessary to pursue their professional goals and take on new challenges by taking ownership of their own learning and development.

Strategies for Upskilling for women:

✓ **Identify your Goals**: Determine your career goals and the skills you need to acquire before starting any upskilling path. Spend some time thinking about your advantages and disadvantages and your growth areas. Make a list of the information and abilities that are most in demand in your industry, then research them.

- ✓ **Network and Look for Mentors**: Building relationships with other professionals who can provide direction and support is essential in any field, but women may find it particularly necessary. Find mentors who can give you constructive criticism on your work, point out areas for improvement, and connect you with people in your profession. To grow your network and keep current on industry news, attend networking events and conferences and join professional organisations and online communities.
- ✓ **Using Opportunities for Professional Development**: Several employers provide professional growth opportunities, including training courses, conferences, and workshops. Use these chances to your advantage to pick up knowledge and develop new abilities that will help you succeed in your job. Consider approaching your supervisor to talk about your objectives and what you need to do to reach them if your workplace doesn't provide these opportunities.
- ✓ **Get More Education**: You can show dedication to your job and learn new skills and information by furthering your education, such as by acquiring a degree or certification. Search for classes or programmes that can fit into your schedule and are flexible, such as online or part-time courses. If money is a problem, look into scholarships or other financing opportunities that can assist with the costs. You can also look for extra training and education opportunities, such as completing online

classes or going after advanced degrees. They can show their dedication to lifelong learning and professional development by participating in these programmes while also gaining new skills and knowledge that are in demand in their industry.

✓ **Participate in New Projects or Initiatives**: Participating in new projects or initiatives can allow you to learn new skills and obtain experiences that can advance your career. Look for chances to mentor individuals in your workplace or assume leadership roles. Volunteering in your field or performing community service can also help you build your network and get helpful experience.

✓ **Keep Current with Industry Trends**: It's critical to stay current on market trends and advancements to maintain your position as a leader in your sector. To remain current on the most recent news and trends, read industry publications, participate in webinars, and participate in online forums. You can use this to pinpoint emerging growth sectors and choose where to concentrate your efforts on upskilling.

Overcome the barriers to upskilling:

Despite the many advantages of upskilling, women may encounter many obstacles that make it more challenging for them to pursue continued learning and development. They can include time restraints, budgetary restrictions, or obligations to one's family that make it difficult to dedicate oneself to further study or training.

Women can look for flexible learning opportunities that enable them to balance their personal and professional duties to get beyond these hurdles. This could entail enrolling in self-paced online classes or looking for training programmes with accommodating schedules or childcare choices.

Also, women can request assistance from their employers through money for further education or training, time off to attend conferences or workshops, or other tools to help them achieve their professional objectives.

I relentlessly support the fantastic value of constant education and upskilling for women. One of the most potent learnings that my dad gave me as a child was:

"A pen is a sword in your hands. It can pick you up from the depths of obscurity to the heights of success."

My dad is so right. Education is the most extraordinary power in the hands of a woman.

In these 40 years of existence, I have built the following skill sets:

1. Biotechnology
2. Meditation and self-healing
3. Research, Monitoring & Evaluation and Learning.
4. Stock Trading and Investments
5. National Institute of Securities Markets (NISM) certified Mutual Fund Distributor.
6. Professional Development strategies and hacks.
7. Book Writing
8. Handwriting Analysis
9. Life Hacking
10. Corporate Training

11. Law of Attraction
12. Neuro Linguistic Programming
13. Digital Coaching
14. Emotional freedom technique (EFT) & Ho'oponopono

Each of these learnings has brought me profits and many new insights. Most importantly, they have kept my brain active. When you learn, you earn. Every new learning has the potential to transform your life at every level. This book is an outcome of all these learnings.

Most importantly, this quest of constant upskilling gave me the strength, power and confidence to grow constantly. These learnings helped me to navigate the world around me in a much-refined way. They have helped me identify what I want from this life and how to get it.

Life has taught me that when a woman brings home an income, her decision-making power increases in the household and her self-confidence increases by leaps and bounds. When this happens, she can assert her security at home like a PowerWoman.

Finding Inner Peace: The Power of Meditation for Women's Mental Health and Well-Being.

In my twenties, I was in a highly toxic relationship with an exploitative man. Although I could see most of the red flags in the relationship, like most women, I used to erroneously think that "I will change him one day". However, one day I found out that he had been cheating on me all this while.

I dropped him like a hot potato the same day I found out.

The ending of a close relationship – Death of a loved one, breakup, job loss, loss of economic security – is a highly traumatic experience for anyone. For a long time, I was messed up emotionally and physically.

During that lowest moment, my friend Hiteshi introduced me to ThetaHealing. I attended the 7-day ThetaHealing on my birthday in July 2016.

In those seven days, I was transformed. My family, friends, reporting manager and colleagues at work told me how much I had changed.

Meditation taught me that I am the Creator of all the magic and mess in my life. When I work hard and push my limits, I create magic. When I pull others down, bitch and gossip against others, I make a mess.

One big mistake is blaming others for our misfortunes and taking credit for and not acknowledging others who helped us attain that success when we are successful.

Meditation helped me see who I truly am. It showed me, through experience, that I am not a human having a spiritual experience, but a spiritual being having a human experience. Most importantly, meditation showed me that my messed up, and disturbed mindset in my teens had brought that toxic, manipulative boyfriend into my life. Learning meditation has helped me take ownership of all bad situations and given me the power to correct myself whenever I am going wrong.

It has also given me the power to focus on the task.

In other words, meditation is a powerful tool to transform any woman into a PowerWoman.

I have been blessed to have been exposed to and learned the following meditation modalities.

1. ThetaHealing[12]
2. Reiki[13]
3. Sahaj Marg's Heartfulness Meditation[14].

Regardless of gender, meditation is a potent tool with many positive effects. But, regular meditation practice may be beneficial for women in tackling their issues.

1. The power of meditation to lessen tension and anxiety is one of its main advantages. Women frequently juggle various jobs and responsibilities, including careers, family responsibilities, and community activity, which can lead to stress and strain. Even a little meditation session each day can help lessen these overwhelming feelings and encourage a peaceful, concentrated state of mind.
2. In addition to improving sleep quality, meditation can benefit women's health and well-being. Insomnia is a common sleep disorder that many women experience, and it can harm their physical and mental health. It may be simpler to get to sleep

---

[12] ThetaHealing method, founded by Ms Vianna Stibal, is a meditation technique and spiritual philosophy that uses focused thought and prayer. During this meditation, we tap into the Theta Brainwaves to access the incredible Source of Energy within us.

[13] Reiki is an alternative therapy that channels life-force energy through gentle touch to promote relaxation and healing. It is believed to help restore balance and harmony within the body, mind, and spirit.

[14] Sahaj Marg's Heartfulness Meditation is a meditation that focuses on the heart, promoting inner peace and balance.

and stay asleep all night if you meditate to calm your mind and relax.

3. The ability of meditation to foster self-awareness and self-compassion in women is another possible benefit of the practice. Women are frequently taught to prioritise the needs of others over their own, which can result in emotions of bitterness and fatigue. Women can tune into their needs and feelings through meditation, developing self-awareness and self-compassion.
4. Moreover, meditation can help women find more meaning and purpose in their lives. Even though they seem to have it all on thc outsidc, many women experience alienation or unhappiness. Women who meditate can access their inner wisdom and intuition, which leads to a greater sense of contentment and purpose.

Meditation may empower women by enabling them to access their inner Resilience and strength. Women encounter various difficulties and barriers in life, including sexism, gender-based violence, and discrimination. Women who practise meditation can develop a sense of inner resilience and strength, which will help them tackle these difficulties with more courage and confidence.

Chapter Summary:

1. We must love ourselves unconditionally to become unable and unavailable to experience gender-based violence.
2. Feeling guilty by a woman who has experienced gender-based violence is folly as she is in no way responsible for that violent

act. Understanding that it's the culprit's fault and no one else's is fundamental.

3. Creating safe spaces in families and communities is necessary to help women experiencing gender-based violence report it to family and authorities.
4. Building a support network of friends is very important towards attaining a long life, reducing stress, belonging to a community and receiving support in challenging situations.
5. Learning to ask for help is an essential skill that women must learn to lead healthier and happier lives.
6. Saving monthly money helps women financially safeguard themselves from rainy days.
7. Constant upskilling helps women to succeed in their careers and attain a sense of empowerment.
8. Meditation helps women find calm within themselves, heal from toxic relationships and promote self-awareness and self-compassion.

CHAPTER 11

STRATEGIES FOR SUCCESS: PRACTICAL APPROACHES TO ACHIEVING YOUR GOALS

PTSD[15] Visualization: For Trauma Relief & Healing

Success in today's fast-paced society is frequently determined by extraneous elements like money, power, and status. In their quest for achievement, women in particular face distinct obstacles like discrimination, gender bias, and cultural expectations.

In the face of these obstacles, many women could feel overburdened and frustrated and wonder whether there is a secret formula or quick fix to attract success. While there isn't a one-size-fits-all approach, there are techniques and practices that women can employ to foster a success-oriented mindset and establish the prerequisites for success.

This chapter will examine the concepts of well researched and proven methods such as gratitude, affirmation, visualization

[15] PTSD: Post Traumatic Stress Disorder.

and techniques like the mirror exercise, Ho'oponopono, listening to Earl Nightingale's Strangest Secret audio as means of attracting success into the lives of women.

Cultivating Gratitude: The Empowering Process of Gratitude Internalization Process

Gratitude is a feeling of appreciation and thankfulness towards something or someone. It's an emotion that can arise from a variety of sources, including the people in our lives, the experiences we've had, and the things we possess. Gratitude is an essential aspect of a fulfilling life, as it enables us to recognise and appreciate the good in our lives, despite the challenges and difficulties we may face.

Practicing gratitude is not just a matter of being polite or courteous; it has real benefits for our mental and physical well-being. Research has shown that people who regularly practise gratitude are happier, more optimistic, and experience less stress and anxiety than those who do not. Gratitude also has positive effects on our relationships, making us more empathetic, forgiving, and supportive of others.

Allow me to share a simple gratitude meditation that I developed on my own and practice daily. This meditation has helped me heal a lot, in terms of developing my inner strength and in helping me forgive the people who have hurt me in the past.

I do this gratitude practice in the morning while commuting to the office, in the evening while returning, also while commuting to my home from the office, and before sleeping at night. It helps me use commuting time constructively.

So, let's go ahead and learn this simple yet incredibly powerful gratitude practice:

Close your eyes and take three deep breaths. While breathing in, count from one to four, and while breathing out, count from one to eight. Breathe out slowly and deeply.

Now take three deep breaths during which you open your mouth as you exhale. Breathe thrice with such open-mouth exhalations.

Now, remember the first instance of someone or something helping you first thing in the morning. I usually visualize the alarm clock that helps me wake up early. I remember the service the alarm clock gave me. This simply illuminates my heart with gratitude. I then simply visualize the clock being engulfed in and transformed into a golden light. I then visualize this golden light getting absorbed into my brain, and as my brain absorbs this golden light, it itself gets illuminated with that same golden light. This is followed by my visualization that my entire body is glowing with that same golden light.

Next, I think about the next person or thing, for e.g. my daughter kissing my cheeks with love. I again think about the act in which my daughter gave me love. This again fills me up with gratitude. I then visualize my daughter becoming engulfed and full of light and entering my brain, brightly illuminating it in the process. This is followed by the visualization of my entire body getting illuminated with that golden light.

I repeat this process until I visualize every person and thing that has served me, even in the minutest of ways, upon waking up till the point I am practising the gratitude exercise.

I call it the **Gratitude Internalization Process**.

The basis of this practice is that we, and everything around us, are made up of energy and vibrations. Love is the highest vibration of them all. Gratitude is one of the infinite forms of Love. I associate the colour gold with Love and so when things and people get illuminated with love and enter my brain, it fills my brain and body with love as well.

This process sends tingling down my being every time I do it.

I encourage you to try this wonderful process and let me know how you find it!

Manifesting Your Dreams: Affirmations and Vision Boards

Two effective methods that women can use to accomplish their goals, increase their drive and confidence, and adopt a more optimistic outlook are affirmations and vision boards.

Affirmations

Positive sentences that you repeat to yourself on a regular basis are known as affirmations. By doing this, you can develop a good outlook and draw favourable circumstances into your life. They operate by reprogramming your subconscious mind and swapping out negative thoughts and beliefs for constructive ones.

Creating Goal-specific affirmations:

An effective technique for attracting your desired results is to formulate affirmations that are targeted towards your goals and feel as though they have already been accomplished. Here is how you do it:

1. <u>Set goals for yourself:</u> Consider your goals for your relationships, health, job, personal development, and finances, among other areas of your life. List your objectives and describe them in the present tense **as if you have already accomplished them**.

For instance:

✓ I have a fulfilling and successful career that brings me happiness and abundance.
✓ I am in a loving and supportive relationship that nourishes my soul.
✓ I am healthy and strong, and my body radiates vitality and energy.
✓ I am financially secure and abundant, and money flows to me effortlessly.
✓ I am a New York Times/ Amazon best-selling author.

2. <u>Don't generalise:</u> Be precise and thorough. Your affirmations' potency will increase with the more precise and thorough they are. Employ evocative language and expressions to arouse a sense of well-being.

For instance:

✓ I am earning $/ Rs. (<u>desired amount of money</u>) every month.

- ✓ I have lost (desired weight loss in pounds/ kgs; eg. 5 kgs) weight by today (date, month and year by which you intend to lose that weight). For eg. "I have lost 5kgs weight by today, 31.12.2023".
- ✓ I have completed this (name of the project) project much before its deadline of (DD/MM/YYYY).
- ✓ I wake up every morning excited to go to work, knowing that I am making a meaningful impact in the world and being rewarded generously for my talents and contributions.
- ✓ My partner and I share a deep connection of trust, respect, and mutual growth. We communicate openly and honestly, and we support each other's dreams and aspirations.
- ✓ I prioritise my health and well-being, and I engage in activities that bring me joy and vitality, such as yoga, hiking, and dancing. My body feels strong, vibrant, and alive.
- ✓ I have a thriving business that provides value and service to my clients, and I am financially rewarded for my expertise and passion. I enjoy abundance and financial freedom, and I use my resources to support causes that align with my values and vision.

3. Regularly repeat them. Repeat your affirmations repeatedly throughout the day to help them stick in your subconscious mind. You can speak them aloud, write them down, or conjure up an image in your head.

Practice them in the following way:

a. Affirmations should be spoken out or quietly to oneself each morning before getting out of bed.

b. Place sticky notes with your affirmations on them and stick them wherever you'll see them frequently, like your computer screen or the mirror in the restroom.
c. Visualize yourself as having already achieved your goals. Put your eyes closed and visualise yourself having attained your goal in that particular scenario. The ability to see oneself, experience one's feelings, and hear one's associated sounds.

Vision Boards

A vision board is a visual representation of your goals, dreams, and aspirations. It's a collage of images, words, and symbols that inspire and motivate you to take action towards achieving your desired outcomes. Vision boards work by activating the law of attraction, which states that like attracts like. By focusing on the things you want to manifest, you attract them into your life.

<u>To create a vision board, you'll need a few supplies:</u>

✓ A large poster board or corkboard
✓ Magazines, newspapers, or printouts of images and words that represent your goals and desires
✓ Scissors, glue, and tape
✓ Markers or stickers (optional)

<u>Here's how to create a vision board:</u>

1. **Set your intentions:** Before you start gathering materials for your vision board, take some time to reflect on your goals and desires. What do you want to achieve in your career, relationships, health, personal growth, and other areas of your

life? Write down your intentions and make them as specific and detailed as possible.

2. **Gather materials:** Look for images, words, and symbols that represent your intentions in magazines, newspapers, or online. Cut out the ones that resonate with you and set them aside.
3. **Arrange the materials on the board:** Start placing the images and words on the board, arranging them in a way that feels visually pleasing and inspiring to you. You can also add personal photos, quotes, or stickers to personalize your board.
4. **Glue or tape the materials in place:** Once you're happy with the arrangement, glue or tape the materials onto the board. You can also use markers or stickers to add extra details or embellishments.
5. **Display and use your vision board:** Once your vision board is complete, display it somewhere you'll see it every day, such as your bedroom or office. Take a few minutes each day to look at your board and visualize yourself achieving your goals. You can also use your board as a tool for setting daily or weekly intentions and tracking your progress towards your desired outcomes.

Self-Reflection: The Empowering Benefits of the Mirror Exercise

A mirror exercise is a powerful tool for self-empowerment and self-improvement. This technique involves looking into a mirror and affirming positive statements about yourself. By using the mirror exercise regularly, you can boost your self-confidence, improve your self-image, and achieve your goals. In this chapter, we will explore the mirror exercise and provide step-by-step instructions on how to use it for self-empowerment.

What is the Mirror Exercise?

The mirror exercise is a self-improvement tool that involves using positive affirmations while looking into a mirror. It is based on the principle of self-talk, which is the internal dialogue that we have with ourselves. The mirror technique helps to change negative self-talk into positive self-talk, which can boost self-confidence and self-esteem.

Steps for Using the Mirror Exercise

1. **Choose a positive affirmation:** The first step in the mirror exercise is to choose a positive affirmation. This affirmation should be a short, positive statement that reflects your desired outcome. For example, if you want to improve your self-confidence, you could choose an affirmation like "I am confident and capable."
2. **Stand in front of a mirror:** Once you have chosen your affirmation, stand in front of a mirror. Make sure that you can see your face clearly.
3. **Look into your own eyes:** Look into your own eyes in the mirror. This can be uncomfortable at first, but it is important to establish a connection with yourself.
4. **Repeat your affirmation:** Repeat your chosen affirmation out loud, while looking into your own eyes in the mirror. Say it slowly and clearly, with conviction and sincerity. Repeat it several times until you feel the words sinking in.

5. **Visualize your desired outcome:** As you repeat your affirmation, visualize your desired outcome. Imagine yourself achieving your goal and experiencing the emotions associated with it. For example, if your affirmation is "I am confident and capable," visualize yourself speaking in front of a group with ease and feeling confident and capable.
6. **Practice regularly:** The mirror technique is a skill that requires practice. Set aside time each day to use the mirror technique, ideally in a quiet and comfortable place. The more you practice, the easier it will become to affirm positive statements about yourself.

Examples of the Mirror Exercise

- ✓ Self-esteem: Use the mirror exercise to boost your self-esteem. Choose an affirmation like "I am worthy and deserving of love and respect," and repeat it while looking into the mirror.
- ✓ Goal achievement: Use the mirror exercise to achieve your goals. Choose an affirmation that reflects your desired outcome, and repeat it while visualizing yourself achieving your goal.
- ✓ Personal growth: Use the mirror exercise to promote personal growth. Choose an affirmation that reflects your desired personal qualities, such as "I am patient and kind," and repeat it while looking into the mirror.

My Favorite Mirror Exercise Affirmation is "**I AM MY OWN SUPERWOMAN**".

The mirror exercise is a powerful tool for self-empowerment and self-improvement. By choosing a positive affirmation, standing in front of a mirror, repeating the affirmation while looking into your own eyes, visualizing your desired outcome, and practicing regularly, you can boost your self-confidence, improve your self-image, and achieve your goals. Use the mirror exercise to promote self-esteem, achieve your goals, and promote personal growth. Start using the mirror exercise today and watch your self-empowerment soar.

Purifying Your Mind and Body: The Empowering Benefits of Blessing Your Drinking Water.

The world around us is composed of 80% water. So are our bodies. Water is essential for our survival, and it plays a crucial role in maintaining our physical and mental health. However, we often take water for granted and forget to appreciate the importance of this life-giving resource. One way to cultivate gratitude and reverence for water is by blessing it before every sip with an affirmation. This is an amazing practice, and it has helped me a lot in taking small, sure steps towards achieving my goals, for e.g. writing my own book.

Steps for Using the Bless the Water Technique:

1. Write down a set of one goal-based affirmation each for the domains of relationships, well-being, job and your finances. For e.g. "I have a loving relationship with my husband" (Relationships), "I have lost 5 kg weight as on dd/mm/yyyy" (well-being), I have been promoted to the position of (desired designation) as on dd/mm/yyyy" (job); and "I am earning (desired amount of money) every month" (finance).

2. Take a glass full of water or a water bottle (if you love to drink water my way!).
3. Before taking a sip of water, say one of those four affirmations. For e.g., say "I have a loving relationship with my husband" and then take your first sip of water. Then say "I have lost 5 kg weight as on dd/mm/yyyy" and take a second sip of water.
4. Continue this way saying an affirmation before taking every sip of water.
5. You can say the same affirmation with every sip of water you take or say different affirmations with every sip – do it your way.
6. Practice this everyday, until it becomes a habit.

The important point to remember here is that **you have to say an affirmation before taking a sip of water**.

This is a magical technique. It works.

Try it out the way I tell you and then let me know your results.

Embracing Forgiveness: The Transformative Practice of Ho'oponopono.

A centuries-old Hawaiian practice known as Ho'oponopono encourages forgiveness and healing within families, communities, and individuals. Ho'oponopono, which means "**to make things right**" or "**to put things in order**," is a practise that involves accepting accountability for one's own thoughts, deeds, and emotions as well as asking for forgiveness for any harm or negative energy that has been inflicted upon oneself or other people.

In this Hawaiian practice, people are encouraged to say "I'm sorry," "Please forgive me," "Thank you," and "I love you," as these words help in attaining peace and also are supposed to speed up healing as per the ancient Hawaiian wisdom.

Principles of this practise:

i. Responsibility: Taking responsibility for your own ideas, feelings, and actions is one of the core concepts of Ho'oponopono. This is realising that you have the ability to modify your inner thoughts and perceptions, which are reflected in your daily experiences.
ii. Forgiveness: Ho'oponopono places a strong emphasis on the necessity of forgiving oneself as well as others. It implores people to express regret for any wrongdoing and ask for pardon, as well as to forgive anyone who has wronged them.
iii. Gratitude: Ho'oponopono places a strong emphasis on the value of showing thanks and appreciation for one's benefits in life. It encourages people to concentrate on the good things in their lives and to foster feelings of joy and thankfulness.
iv. Love: According to Ho'oponopono, love is the most potent force in the cosmos and has the ability to heal even the most serious wounds. It promotes people to develop feelings of compassion and love for both themselves and other people.
v. Letting Go: Ho'oponopono places a strong emphasis on the necessity of letting go of unfavourable thoughts, feelings, and beliefs. It exhorts people to let go of any bad energy they might be hanging onto and to exchange it for uplifting energy.

Where can Ho'oponopono be applied:

Ho'oponopono can be used in a range of situations, from intimate relationships to the workplace.

- ✓ **Personal relationships:** Whether with love partners, family members, or friends, Ho'oponopono can be utilized to mend and enhance personal relationships. We can establish more meaningful connections with others around us by taking ownership of our own ideas and feelings, asking for forgiveness, and nurturing feelings of love and gratitude.
- ✓ **Health & wellness:** By letting go of negative energy and nurturing feelings of love and gratitude, Ho'oponopono can be used to enhance our physical and mental well-being. Those who are dealing with chronic illnesses, anxiety, or depression may find it very beneficial.
- ✓ **Work and careers:** By letting go of bad energy, accepting accountability for our own thoughts and deeds, and nurturing feelings of love and gratitude for both ourselves and others, Ho'oponopono can be utilized to enhance our professional connections and career success.
- ✓ **Global events:** World events such as war, hunger, and environmental degradation, can also be addressed using Ho'oponopono. We can help create a more tranquil and harmonious environment by accepting responsibility for our own thoughts and deeds, asking for forgiveness, and nurturing feelings of love and gratitude.

How can one practice Ho'oponopono:

So, are you ready to practice this powerful healing technique? Let's do it together.

1. *Identify a person or situation that is giving you stress.* For eg. **Person**: Suppose you are feeling resentful towards your Mom or your Boss. **Situation**: Suppose you are worried about your job interview or you are worried about your own/ your child's exam.
2. *Think about that person or situation and say this four-statement mantra with me*:
   a. I am sorry (person/situation).
   b. Please forgive me (person/situation).
   c. Thank you (person/situation).
   d. I love you (person/situation).

3. *Repeat the I am sorry* (person/situation), *Please forgive me* (person/situation), *Thank You* (person/situation), *I Love You* (person/situation) *four-statement mantra* **9 times**.
4. *I find this technique to be highly effective when I chant this four-statement mantra* **108 (1+0+8 = 9) times.** I use a prayer bead to chant the four-statement mantra 108 times. I personally do it 108 times. You could do it as many times as you wish. 108 is a random number that I chose.
5. *At one time, you can practice Ho'oponopono only on a SINGLE PERSON OR SITUATION.*
6. *Practice Ho'oponopono at least twice a day (for two persons/ two situation/ one person-one situation)*

I practice Ho'oponopono twice daily and it has helped me achieve incredible results. The key to the effectiveness of this practice is supreme belief in it. Now that you believe in this practice, please do it twice daily. That's my humble request.

Seeing is Believing: The Transformative Power of Visualization Techniques

Visualization is a powerful tool that can help you manifest your goals and achieve success.

What is Visualization?

Visualization is a technique that involves creating a mental image of what you want to achieve. It involves using your imagination to create a vivid picture of your goal, including the details and emotions associated with it. By visualizing your goal, you can train your mind to focus on the positive outcome and attract it into your life.

Steps for Visualization

1. **Set a clear goal**: The first step in visualization is to set a clear goal. Your goal should be specific, measurable, achievable, relevant, and time-bound (SMART). For example, if your goal is to start a business, you should define what type of business you want to start, how much money you need to invest, and when you want to launch it.
2. **Create a mental image**: Once you have set your goal, close your eyes, and create a mental image of what it looks like. Imagine yourself already achieving your goal and experiencing the emotions associated with it. For example, if your goal is to start a business, visualize yourself in your office, meeting with clients, and making money.
3. **Use your senses**: As you visualize your goal, engage all your senses to make it more real. Imagine the sights, sounds, smells,

tastes, and sensations associated with achieving your goal. For example, if your goal is to travel to a tropical island, imagine the feel of the warm sand on your toes, the sound of the ocean waves, the smell of the salty air, and the taste of a refreshing drink.

4. **Practice regularly**: Visualization is a skill that requires practice. Set aside time each day to visualize your goal, ideally in a quiet and comfortable place. The more you practice, the easier it will become to create a vivid mental image of your goal.

Examples of Visualization

- <u>Athletes</u>: Athletes use visualization to enhance their performance. They visualize themselves performing their sport at the highest level and experiencing the emotions associated with winning. For example, a runner may visualize themselves crossing the finish line in first place and feeling the excitement of winning.
- <u>Business professionals</u>: Business professionals use visualization to achieve their goals. They visualize themselves achieving their business objectives, such as closing a deal or launching a new product. For example, a salesperson may visualize themselves making a successful pitch to a client and signing a contract.
- <u>Health and wellness</u>: People use visualization to improve their health and well-being. They visualize themselves being healthy, fit, and happy. For example, someone trying to lose weight may visualize themselves in their ideal body, feeling confident and healthy.

Visualization is a powerful tool that can help you manifest your goals and achieve success. By setting a clear goal, creating a mental image, engaging your senses, and practicing regularly, you can train your mind to focus on the positive outcome and attract it into your life. Use visualization to enhance your performance, achieve your business objectives, and improve your health and well-being. Start visualizing your goals today and watch them become a reality.

Earl Nightingale's The Strangest Secret: Unlocking the Power Within.

I first heard this magical masterpiece around 3 years ago. Earl Nightingale's voice is enough to force you to get up and take action.Today, I have started two companies and am an author.

This amazing video has created millions of entrepreneurs, billions of dollars and trillions of opportunities.

Listen to this video once every day for at least 30 days and experience the magic yourself.

"The Strangest Secret" is a motivational speech that has inspired millions of people around the world to live their best lives. In this chapter, we will explore the history of this iconic speech and how it came to be.

Earl Nightingale

Earl Nightingale was an American motivational speaker and author who was born in 1921 in Los Angeles, California. He served in the United States Marine Corps during World War II, and after the war, he began a career in radio broadcasting.

In 1956, Nightingale recorded "The Strangest Secret," a motivational speech that he created to help people achieve success and fulfillment in their lives. The speech was originally intended to be a record album that people could listen to in the comfort of their own homes.

"The Strangest Secret"

"The Strangest Secret" is a 30-minute speech that focuses on the power of thoughts and the importance of taking responsibility for our own lives. In the speech, Nightingale argues that our thoughts determine our reality, and that by changing our thoughts, we can change our lives.

The speech became an instant success and was soon distributed across the country as a record album. It was also adapted into a book, which has sold millions of copies around the world.

Legacy

"The Strangest Secret" has had a lasting impact on the field of personal development and has inspired countless people to live their best lives. Its message of taking responsibility for one's own life and focusing on positive thoughts and actions has resonated with people around the world.

Nightingale went on to create a successful career as a motivational speaker and author, and he continued to inspire people with his message of personal growth and development until his death in 1989.

Two steps to turn around your life through the "Strangest Secret"

1. Open the "Earl Nightingale - The Strangest Secret" video on YouTube using the url: https://youtu.be/GKdBxhmb1zY

QR code to view Earl Nightingale's "The Strangest Secret"

2. Hear it at least once daily.

"The Strangest Secret" is a timeless classic that continues to inspire people around the world to live their best lives. Its message of taking responsibility for one's own life and focusing on positive thoughts and actions is as relevant today as it was when it was first created. As we continue on our own journey towards personal growth and development, let us remember the wisdom of Nightingale's words and use them to create the life we truly desire.

Chapter Summary:

1. Gratitude is the key to living happy and fulfilling lives. The Gratitude Internalization Process is a 5-minute practice that can have a profound impact in your life.

2. Affirmations and Vision Boards are two tools that women can use to achieve their goals, boost their confidence and become more optimistic.
3. The Mirror Exercise is a powerful self-improvement and self-empowerment technique.
4. The technique of blessing the water before drinking it helps us constantly stay connected to our goals every time we drink water.
5. Ho'oponopono is a powerful tool encouraging forgiveness and healing within families, communities, and individuals.
6. Daily visualization helps you manifest your goals and grow rapidly in life.
7. Hearing "The Strangest Secret", a motivational speech of Earl Nightingale, at least once daily can have a profound impact on your life.

CHAPTER 12

EMPOWERING CHANGE: STRATEGIES FOR MAKING THE WORLD SAFER FOR WOMEN EVERYWHERE

Voices of Strength: Inspiring Stories of Women

While delivering one of her TEDx talks, Rita met her soulmate Rahul, who had organised that TEDx talk. She immediately connected with him, dated him for 3 years and then married him.

One year after marrying Rahul, Rita was blessed with a beautiful baby girl named Riddhi. As a mother, Rita was determined to give her daughter the love, support, and guidance she needed to grow into an empowered and independent woman.

From a young age, Rita instilled in Riddhi a sense of self-confidence and a belief in her abilities. She encouraged her to pursue her interests and passions, whether music, sports, or academics. She also taught her the importance of standing up for herself and speaking out against injustice.

As Riddhi grew older, Rita became a positive role model and source of inspiration. She encouraged her to pursue higher education and helped her to secure a scholarship to study abroad. Despite the challenges of being away from home, Riddhi excelled in her studies and graduated with honours.

With her mother's support and guidance, Riddhi became a successful entrepreneur and a strong advocate for women's rights. She started a company that focused on empowering women and providing them with the necessary resources to succeed in business. She also volunteered her time and resources to support organisations that worked to end gender-based violence and discrimination. ***(CONCLUDED)***

The safety and well-being of women are fundamental human rights that should be protected and upheld by societies worldwide. However, gender-based violence and discrimination continue to be significant issues that affect women and girls across the globe. From domestic violence and sexual assault to forced marriage and honour killings, women face numerous daily threats to their safety and dignity.

In this chapter, we will explore how we can work to make the world a safer place for women. We will examine education and awareness-raising initiatives' role in preventing gender-based violence and empowering women. We will discuss strategies for promoting gender equality and challenging harmful cultural norms and attitudes perpetuating violence and discrimination.

This chapter will provide readers with a better understanding of the steps that can be taken to make the world safe for women.

Whether through legal action, education, or advocacy, we all have a role in creating a world where women can live free from violence and discrimination.

DID YOU KNOW:

There are many inspiring stories of women who have been supported and empowered by their families while growing up and in their marital families. Here are a few examples:

Michelle Obama*: Michelle Obama, the former First Lady of the United States, credits her parents and family for providing her with the support and encouragement she needed to achieve her goals. Despite facing racism and discrimination throughout her life, Michelle went on to attend Princeton University and Harvard Law School and later became an advocate for education and health initiatives during her time as First Lady.*

Sheryl Sandberg*: Sheryl Sandberg, the COO of Facebook and author of "Lean In," has spoken publicly about the support she received from her husband and family as she pursued her career in technology. She credits their encouragement and understanding for allowing her to succeed and break through the glass ceiling in the male-dominated tech industry.*

Ellen DeGeneres*: Ellen DeGeneres, a comedian and television host, came out as gay in the 1990s and faced backlash and discrimination. However, she has credited her wife, Portia de Rossi, for providing her with the love and support she needed to overcome these challenges and continue pursuing her career. She has also used* *her platform to advocate for LGBTQ+ rights and other social justice issues.*

***Mindy Kaling**: Mindy Kaling, a writer, comedian, and actress, has spoken publicly about the support she received from her family as she pursued her career in the entertainment industry. She has credited her parents for encouraging her creativity and instilling the confidence to pursue her dreams, despite facing barriers as a woman of colour in Hollywood.*

***Aishwarya Rai Bachchan**: Aishwarya Rai Bachchan, a Bollywood actress and former Miss World, has credited her family with the support and encouragement she needed to pursue her dreams. Despite criticism and backlash for her career choices and personal life, Aishwarya has remained committed to her craft. She has used her platform to advocate for various social causes, including HIV/AIDS awareness and eye donation.*

Women Empowering Women: Strategies for Safety and Empowerment

Violence against women is a complex and multi-faceted problem that requires a comprehensive response. Women have led the movement at the forefront to end gender-based violence, organising, speaking out, and supporting survivors. This chapter will explore women's strategies to promote safety and empowerment, including organising for change, speaking out against violence, and supporting survivors.

Organising Change

Organising change is one of the women's most potent tools to promote safety and empowerment. Women's organisations have been instrumental in raising awareness about the issue of gender-based violence and advocating for policies and programs that support survivors and prevent violence from occurring first and foremost.

Women's organisations can take many forms, from grassroots groups to large-scale international organisations. Grassroots groups often work locally, organising rallies and protests, providing support services to survivors, and advocating for policy changes. Large-scale organisations, such as the United Nations Entity for Gender Equality and the Empowerment of Women (UN Women), work globally to promote gender equality and women's empowerment.

Women's organisations have been instrumental in securing legal protections for women, such as laws against domestic violence and sexual assault. They have also been effective in raising awareness about the issue of gender-based violence and promoting a cultural shift towards more tremendous respect for women's rights.

Speaking Out Against Violence

Speaking out against violence is another strategy women have used to promote safety and empowerment. Women have been vocal about their experiences of violence, sharing their stories in public forums and social media. By speaking out, women have been able to break the silence surrounding gender-based violence and raise awareness about the prevalence of the problem.

Speaking out against violence can also have a therapeutic effect on survivors, helping them to overcome the shame and guilt associated with their experiences. By sharing their stories, survivors can connect with others who have had similar experiences and find a sense of solidarity and support.

Supporting Survivors

Supporting survivors is another critical strategy women have used to promote safety and empowerment. Women's organisations and community groups have provided various support services to survivors, including counselling, legal advocacy, and emergency shelter.

Supporting survivors is essential because it helps ensure they are not re-victimised by the criminal justice system or their abusers. It also allows survivors to heal from their experiences and trauma and regain control over their lives.

Women have lead the movement to end gender-based violence, using various strategies to promote safety and empowerment. Organising for change, speaking out against violence, and supporting survivors are just a few of the methods that have been effective in raising awareness about the problem of violence against women and advocating for policy changes. As we work towards a world free from gender-based violence, we must support and empower women to take action and create change.

Partnering for Change: The Role of Men as Allies in the Fight Against Gender-Based Violence

While women have been at the forefront of the movement to end gender-based violence, men also have a very important role in the creation of a safer and more equitable world. In this chapter, we will explore how men can become allies in the fight against gender-based violence.

Challenging Gender Stereotypes

One of the most critical ways men can become allies is by **challenging gender stereotypes.** Traditional gender roles and expectations can contribute to a culture of violence against women by perpetuating harmful ideas about masculinity and femininity.

Men can challenge these stereotypes by rejecting the idea that violence is acceptable to assert power or control over others. They can also work to create more inclusive and equitable spaces where people of all genders are valued and respected.

Supporting Women's Leadership

Another way in which men can become allies is by **supporting women's leadership**. Women's organisations have been instrumental in advocating for policy changes and providing support services to survivors of gender-based violence. Men can help these organisations by donating time or resources or amplifying the voices of women leaders in their communities.

Men can also **ensure that women's voices are heard and respected in all areas of society**, including in the workplace, politics, and the media. By working with women to create more inclusive and equitable spaces, men can help promote gender equality and prevent gender-based violence.

Intervening in Harmful Behaviors

Men can also become allies by **intervening in harmful behaviours**. This means speaking out when they witness sexist or violent behaviour, whether it is directed at women or other men. By holding themselves and others accountable for their actions, men can help to create a culture of respect and nonviolence.

Men can also take steps to **prevent harmful behaviours from occurring in the first place**. This includes promoting healthy relationships, teaching young people about consent, and respecting boundaries. By taking an active role in preventing gender-based violence, men can help to create a safer and more equitable world for everyone.

Men have a very important role to play in the fight against gender-based violence. By challenging gender stereotypes, supporting women's leadership, and intervening in harmful behaviours, men can help to create a culture of respect and nonviolence. As we work towards a world free from gender-based violence, it is essential that men and women work together as allies to create change.

Empowering the Next Generation: Raising Strong and Confident Daughters.

My daughter is my Goddess. She has been treated like a VIP in my marital family, and I am grateful for that. The impact of this VIP treatment is that she has crushed all her developmental milestones. She also secured admission to the Nursery section of her School in Delhi-NCR on her own. We, her parents, just went there as her accessories. I know she is a rockstar, and she will surpass all I have achieved. My daughter is my pride.

As parents, it should be our top priority to want the best for our daughters. We want them to be successful and in good health. So, what does it mean to give your daughter real power? And how can you support her in gaining the self-esteem, resiliency, and confidence she needs to face life's challenges?

Here are some key strategies for empowering our daughters and helping them reach their full potential:

- ☐ **Encourage Her:** Encouraging your daughter to follow her passions is one of the most vital things you can do to give your daughter confidence. Whether she enjoys science, music, art, or athletics, encouraging her interests can give her a sense of direction and purpose. When she develops new talents and pushes herself, it can also help her increase her sense of confidence and self-worth.
- ☐ **Modelling good self-Esteem**: One of your daughter's most significant role models is you as a parent. You may encourage your daughter to develop positive self-esteem and self-care habits by setting an example for them. This entails being

friendly and compassionate to yourself, placing a high priority on your health, and establishing boundaries as required. Your daughter will also learn to value herself when she observes that you regard yourself and your wants.

- ☐ **Show Her How to Accept Failure**: Although failure is a necessary part of life, many kids are trained to fear it. Teach your daughter to view failure as an opportunity for growth if you wish to empower her. Encourage her to try new things and take chances immediately, even if she fails. Honour her efforts and assist her in understanding that making mistakes is a natural part of learning.
- ☐ **Encourage a healthy body self-image:** It's crucial to encourage a positive body self-image and self-acceptance in a society that frequently places a strong emphasis on physical beauty. This involves educating your daughter to cherish her body for its capabilities rather than appearance. Urge her to exercise while emphasising her health and well-being more than her size or weight.
- ☐ **Promote enduring connections:** Good relationships are crucial to wellbeing, and your daughter's relationships will significantly impact how confident and self-assured she feels about herself. Help her to form close bonds with loved ones who will stand by her and lift her up. Teach her how to successfully communicate, establish limits, and constructively settle disputes.
- ☐ **Enrolling her in a self-defence class:** Providing your daughter with self-defence training is an excellent method to make her feel secure and in charge of her protection. She will acquire the knowledge and attitude required to defend herself from

prospective dangers by being taught the fundamentals of self-defence and encouraged to practise frequently. Moreover, self-defence instruction can instill a positive self-image in your daughter and make her feel more confident and assertive in challenging circumstances. Learning self-defence is a great way to give your daughter the confidence to take responsibility for her security and wellbeing.

Building Strong Relationships: Loving and Supporting Your Daughters-in-Law.

My mother-in-law is my Rock, and I am blessed to have her. She loved and cared for me just like any mother ('Ma') would have done during her own daughter's pregnancy. And for this, I shall be grateful to her till my last breath. She treats me like a daughter and not my daughter-in-law.

You may think that how will I understand the conflicts between their mother-in-law and daughter-in-law?

Both my mother and my mother-in-law had challenging relationships with their respective mothers-in-law. I have heard their experiences and admired them for their strength. They made a choice from those bad experiences. They chose to not subject their daughter-in-laws to the kind of experiences they themselves had.

Many mother-in-law and daughter-in-law relationships are based on resentment and mistrust. In many cultures, the relationship between a mother and daughter-in-law can be complex and tense. However, it is vital for both parties to work towards a positive and supportive relationship, as this can significantly impact the well-being and happiness of the entire family.

Here are certain tips towards replacing resentment with love in mother-in-law and daughter-in-law relationships:

- ☐ **Understanding the Need for Acceptance**: A daughter-in-law is an important family member and should be treated respectfully and kindly. A mother-in-law needs to recognise the need for her daughter-in-law to feel accepted and loved. This is especially true when the daughter-in-law is new to the family or is from a different cultural background. Feeling accepted and welcomed by her new family can make a big difference in how the daughter-in-law perceives her place in the family and her relationship with her spouse.
- ☐ **Building Trust and Respect:** Building trust and respect is critical to a healthy relationship between a mother-in-law and daughter-in-law. Both parties should try to communicate openly and honestly with each other. This can involve discussing expectations and boundaries and expressing appreciation and gratitude for each other's contributions to the family.
- ☐ **Showing Kindness and Empathy**: A mother-in-law can show kindness and empathy towards her daughter-in-law by being supportive and understanding. This can involve offering help with childcare or household chores or simply lending a listening ear when the daughter-in-law needs someone to talk to. The mother-in-law must remember that her daughter-in-law may be experiencing challenges and stresses that are unique to her and to offer support and encouragement when needed.

- ☐ **Respecting Differences**: A mother-in-law must respect the differences between herself and her daughter-in-law. This can involve respecting differences in cultural traditions or beliefs, as well as differences in parenting styles or personal preferences. It is essential to recognise that there is no "right" way to do things and that each person brings their unique perspective and experiences to the family.
- ☐ **Setting Boundaries**: While building a positive and supportive relationship between a mother-in-law and daughter-in-law is essential, it is also crucial to set boundaries and respect each other's privacy. This can involve respecting each other's personal space and time and refraining from giving unsolicited advice or criticism. It is essential to remember that everyone has their own way of doing things and that it is okay for there to be differences in opinion or approach.

Leadership Redefined: Becoming an Empathetic and Empowering Women Leader

My first toxic boss in my professional career was a Lady Boss at the National AIDS Control Organization who got so worked up once for a flimsy event that she ordered an elaborate termination exercise for my ouster. At NACO, new recruits were supposed to get their performance reviewed after six months of probation. She ordered my review and termination three months after my joining because I had left her alone for five minutes!

My colleague at NACO helped me combat this situation, and I ultimately won, and she had to leave.

However, I experienced this Queen Bee Syndrome two more times, and now I am positively wary of female bosses. I feel safer around male bosses.

Queen Bee Syndrome is a phenomenon that occurs *when a female boss or manager displays negative behaviour towards other women in the workplace, particularly those who are also in positions of power or authority*. The term "queen bee" is used to describe women who have been successful in their careers but may not be supportive of other women who are trying to do the same.

This behaviour can manifest in various ways, including *belittling or undermining other women, withholding information or opportunities, or creating a hostile or competitive work environment*. It can be a result of various factors, including <u>social and cultural conditioning, fear of losing power or influence, or a belief that women need to compete for scarce opportunities</u>.

The impact of queen bee syndrome can be significant for those who experience negative behaviour and the workplace culture. It can cause a *lack of trust and cooperation among colleagues, decreased morale and job satisfaction, and a failure to promote diversity and inclusion in the workplace*.

There are several plausible explanations for why queen bee syndrome exists. One theory suggests that women who have been successful in male-dominated fields *may feel threatened by other women who could potentially challenge their position*. Another idea is that women who have achieved success *may feel isolated and alone, leading them to act defensively towards other women*.

Regardless of the reason, the negative behaviour associated with queen bee syndrome can have severe consequences for women in the workplace. It can perpetuate stereotypes and gender biases, create a culture of fear and mistrust, and ultimately hinder the success of women as a whole.

It is crucial to recognise the problem and address it directly with the individuals involved to address queen bee syndrome. Training and coaching programs that promote effective leadership and teamwork can help create a more supportive and inclusive workplace culture. It is also essential to ensure that company policies and practices promote diversity and inclusion and to foster an environment where all employees are encouraged to work together to achieve common goals.

All my Queen Bee Bosses have helped me realise that I want to become an empathetic and empowering female boss. For me, my team is my family and not my punching bag. My team believes in and trusts me because I give them sole credit when they burn the midnight oil. I consider it a crime to eat away credit. I develop and attain success when my team grows and achieves a milestone.

Becoming an empathetic and empowering female boss involves developing key leadership skills and cultivating a positive and inclusive workplace culture. Here are some strategies that can help:

- ☐ **Develop self-awareness**: As a leader, it's essential to understand your own emotions and how they impact others. This involves developing emotional intelligence and self-awareness, which can be done through reflection, feedback, and coaching.

- ☐ **Practice active listening**: Active listening involves focusing fully on what the person in front is saying without any interruption or judgement. This skill can help you better understand your employees' perspectives, needs, and concerns and make them feel heard and valued.
- ☐ **Foster a positive workplace culture:** Create a culture that values diversity, inclusion, and mutual respect. Encourage teamwork, collaboration, and open communication, and establish policies and practices that support these values.
- ☐ **Provide feedback and support:** Regular feedback and support can help your employees feel valued and empowered. Offer constructive feedback, recognise their achievements, and provide opportunities for growth and development.
- ☐ **Lead by example:** As a leader, your behaviour sets the example for the rest of the team. Model the behaviour you want to see, such as active listening, respect, and inclusivity, and hold yourself accountable for your actions and decisions.
- ☐ **Empower your employees:** Encourage them to take ownership of their work, make decisions, and express their opinions. Give them the support and resources they require to succeed and create a sense of autonomy and empowerment.
- ☐ **Seek to understand your employees' needs:** Every employee has unique needs and challenges. Take the time to understand your employees' individual circumstances and tailor your leadership approach accordingly.

Chapter Summary:

1. Women-led strategies such as organising for change, speaking out against violence and supporting survivors are essential towards promoting safety and empowerment.
2. By challenging gender stereotypes, supporting women's leadership and intervening in harmful behaviours, men can play their role as allies in the fight against gender-based violence.
3. Empowering our daughters to help them reach their highest potential should be our prime priority as parents. This is crucial to their developing the self-confidence required to overcome the negative impacts of patriarchy.
4. A supportive and positive mother-in-law and daughter-in-law relationship is vital to a healthy and happy family.
5. Female bosses must overcome the desire to adopt the Queen Bee Syndrome and become empathetic and empower female bosses to support other women in their professional lives.

CHAPTER 13

CONCLUSION: FROM BEHIND LOCKED DOORS TO OPEN HEARTS

Twenty-five years ago, in the darkness of that fateful night, a fourteen-year-old girl delivered a resounding kick. That single act of defiance didn't just end a moment of violence. It sparked something much bigger-a lifelong journey toward understanding, healing, and empowerment. Today, as I stand on the other side of that pain, I write this conclusion with a grateful heart and genuine hope for change. This book, *Beyond the Locked Doors: Women's Safety at Home*, is my story. It's also a call-an invitation for all of us to transform together.

Nature's Gift vs. Society's Prison

Throughout these chapters, we've taken a journey that starts with nature itself. And here's what nature is trying to tell us: women are not the "weaker sex." Society says that. Biology says something very different.

Science shows us the truth. Female foetuses survive adversities that would be fatal to male foetuses. Women's bodies create life-an undeniable miracle. Yet we treat it as ordinary, expected, something women simply "do." Women outlive men. We carry genetic advantages that have kept our species thriving for millennia.

So here's the contradiction that keeps me up at night: nature gave women incredible strength and resilience. Yet we've built a social system that works against us. We've created a structure that controls women, limits them, and tells them they should accept less than they deserve.

The Paradox We Can't Ignore

There's a stark truth hiding here: biology blesses us with strength, but society tries to imprison us with expectations.

We explored patriarchy throughout this book-not as something men invented to hurt us, but as a system all of us inherited. And here's the hardest part: women have become gatekeepers of this very system. We police each other. We reinforce the same harmful stereotypes. We pass down generations of suppression, wrapping it in words like "tradition" and "love."

But men suffer too. Patriarchy denies them the freedom to be vulnerable, to cry, to be truly compassionate and human.

This is why the fight isn't women against men. It's all of us against a broken system that steals from all our humanity.

The Numbers That Should Wake Us Up

Let me be honest about what we're facing. The statistics are devastating:

Almost one in three women worldwide has experienced violence-physical or sexual.

Over 86% of that violence comes from the people who should protect us most: husbands, partners, family members.

Every single hour, five women or girls are killed by someone in their own family

Yet most women don't reach out for help. Do you know why? Fear. Shame. The way our culture teaches us to suffer quietly. And a question that haunts survivors: "Will anyone actually believe me? Will they really help?"

Silence is the food that violence feeds on.

In these chapters, we learned to spot the warning signs-all 54 of them. From bruises you can see to the invisible control that slowly erases who you are. We talked about abuse in all its forms: physical, emotional, sexual, financial, psychological. Some abuse is obvious. Some whispers itself in the language of love.

Knowledge Alone Isn't Enough-We Need Action

But here's what I want you to understand: knowing about abuse doesn't protect anyone. We have to act.

This book gives you a real roadmap. Create safety plans. Learn your legal rights. Find the resources that can help. Build your support system. Invest in yourself and keep learning. Most importantly, refuse to accept anything less than respect and dignity.

In India, we're fortunate to have real support structures. One-Stop Centers exist. Mission Shakti and Beti Bachao Beti Padhao are working on the ground. We have the Protection of Women from Domestic Violence Act. We have laws against sexual assault. Around the world, movements like Ni Una Menos, HeForShe, and the 16 Days of Activism are creating momentum.

These aren't just policies sitting in files. They're real declarations that say: women matter. Your safety matters.

What Real Empowerment Actually Looks Like

Now, let me tell you about true empowerment-because I think we've gotten it wrong in a lot of ways.

Real empowerment isn't something someone gives you. You have to claim it for yourself. It looks like this:

Loving yourself completely, even when abuse has planted shame and guilt inside you. Learning to meditate and dream bigger. Believing in your own worth before anyone else does. Saving money-not for someone else's dreams, but for your freedom. Upskilling yourself and refusing to let anyone convince you that you're not capable. Speaking up, asking for help, despite all the voices telling you to stay quiet and suffer.

And here's something crucial that I've learned: empowerment isn't a solo journey.

I've worked with survivors for nearly twenty years, and they've taught me that real healing happens within community. It happens when you're surrounded by women who believe you, who've walked where you've walked, who take your hand and say, "You're not the first. You won't suffer alone."

Empowerment also means how we raise our daughters. It's about supporting our daughters-in-law like they're our own. It's about men becoming true allies-not heroes swooping in to save us, but genuine partners fighting alongside us.

I Want to Speak Directly to You

You're reading this because something inside you recognised that this book matters. Maybe you're a woman trapped in an abusive situation, searching desperately for a way out. Maybe you're worried about someone you love and don't know how to help. Maybe you're a professional working every day to end abuse. Maybe you're a man trying to understand how you can be part of the solution.

Whoever you are, I'm speaking to you now.

To women experiencing abuse:

What's happening to you is not your fault. The shame belongs to the person who chose to hurt you, not to you. I know it feels impossible to leave. I know the world seems designed to keep you trapped. But I also know-from my own life and from thousands of women I've supported-that freedom exists on the other side. Safety is real. A life where you wake without fear, where you make your own choices, where you're truly free-it's possible.

Start somewhere small. Make one phone call. Call 181 (the One Stop Centre helpline in India) or find the resources at the end of this book. Tell someone you trust. Create a safety plan. You don't need anyone's permission to protect yourself.

To families and communities:

Violence feeds on silence. It thrives because we turn away. It survives because we convince ourselves it's "family business."

When you see the warning signs, speak up. When a woman comes to you with unexplained injuries, with fear in her eyes, with a story that doesn't add up-believe her. Protect her. Connect her with help. The Bell Bajao campaign says it perfectly: ring the bell. Interrupt the cycle. Refuse to be silent.

To the men reading this:

Thank you. Just by reading this book, you're already taking a step. Please know that challenging patriarchy isn't about losing anything. It's about finding yourself. It's about teaching your sons to respect women, not control them. It's about freeing yourself from the cage of "being a man" in the way society demands.

History remembers the truly powerful men differently. The ones we respect are those who protected the vulnerable, honored everyone's dignity, and refused to use their strength to dominate. Be that man.

To the professionals and activists:

I see you. I know this work is hard. Some days, progress feels impossibly slow. But I promise you-it matters. Every woman you help, every campaign you run, every policy you push for, every abuser you hold accountable-it creates ripples you'll never fully see.

Here's something powerful: the eight-thousand-year-old Indus Valley Civilization was built on a matriarchal foundation. Its cities were masterpieces. When women led, when their voices mattered, society flourished. We can build that world again.

My Journey, Your Beginning

That night I delivered that kick, I couldn't have imagined where it would lead. I didn't know I'd eventually work with millions of women. I didn't know I'd find my purpose. I couldn't have dreamed of my husband-a man who respects me completely, celebrates my dreams, and partners with me equally. I couldn't have known that my shame would become wisdom, that betrayal would transform into compassion, that pain would fuel purpose.

But twenty-five years later, I understand something essential: Resilience is built into our biology. Agency-that's something we have to claim for ourselves. Nature gave us the blueprint. Now it's our job to build a world that honors that gift instead of destroying it.

This Is Not an Ending-It's a Beginning

This book isn't where the story ends. It's where yours begins.

It's the start of conversations we need to have. Of boundaries we need to set. Of systems we need to tear down and rebuild. Of communities we need to strengthen.

It's a call that says: Beyond locked doors and behind closed walls, women deserve to feel safe. In homes where respect replaces control. In relationships where love means support, not surveillance. In societies where women's voices lead-we can all truly live.

To the People I Love

Mom-Indira Misra-you loved me fiercely. You taught me what real strength looks like. This book is your legacy.

Robin, my husband, you showed me that men can be respectful partners. Thank you for believing in this work.

Rishika, my daughter, you'll grow up in a different world than I did. I'm raising you knowing you're a VIP in your own life. You're a rockstar, and the world is waiting for your brilliance.

To Every Reader Here

You've stayed with me through these pages. Maybe something shifted inside you while reading. Maybe you recognised yourself or someone you love in these stories.

Know this: you are not alone.

We're standing at a turning point together. What we do right now, how we respond to what we've learned, whether we choose to act-it will determine what world we leave for our daughters and sons.

This conclusion isn't really an ending. It's an invitation to your next chapter. As you close this book, ask yourself:

Will I go back to life exactly as it was? Or will I take even one idea from these pages and let it change me? Will I protect one woman? Will I support one survivor? Will I challenge one harmful stereotype? Will I raise my daughter knowing her worth? Will I teach my son to respect?

I really do hope this book moves you to take action and make a real difference. Your support, your engagement with these ideas-it means everything to me. But honestly, what will change everything is your commitment to safety, to justice, to a world where women are truly free.

Beyond locked doors awaits freedom. **Shall we walk through them together?**

A NOTE TO THE READERS

Hi Readers,

Thank you for encouraging me by buying and reading this book.

I care very deeply about this subject. Hope you had some takeaways from this book.

If you liked this book, kindly leave a good rating on Amazon and Goodreads.

I would love to hear from you as to what you thought about this book. Please send me an email at

gunjika.learns@gmail.com or gunjika.misra@gmail.com

Please do consider following me on these channels:

1. LinkedIn
   https://in.linkedin.com/in/gunjikam/
2. Instagram:
   https://www.instagram.com/gunjika/
3. Facebook:

   a) Profile page: https://www.facebook.com/share/19ATE94Fuy/
   b) Author page: https://www.facebook.com/share/1Bepfrpwcj/

Yours Sincerely

Gunjika V Misra

ANNEXURES: SUPPORT RESOURCES FOR VICTIM OF DOMESTIC ABUSE

Annexure A: National Helplines and Resources in India

1. Primary Emergency Helplines

Service	Contact Number	Availability	Services
Women Helpline 181	181 (Toll-free)	24/7	Emergency response, referral to police, OSC, hospitals, legal aid, counselling
NCW Women Helpline	14490 (Toll-free)	24/7	Digital complaint registration, psychological counselling, referral to authorities
NCW Alternative Helpline	7827170170	24/7	Online support, linking with police, hospitals, legal services, psychological counsellors
Police Emergency	100 or 112	24/7	Immediate emergency assistance, police response
Women in Distress	1091 (Toll-free)	24/7	Support and referral services for women

2. One Stop Centres (OSCs)

Overview: One-Stop Centers provide integrated support under one roof including:

- Emergency response and rescue services
- Medical assistance
- Legal aid and counselling
- Psycho-social support and counselling
- Temporary shelter
- Video conferencing facilities for accessing support remotely

How to Access: Walk in to your nearest OSC or call 181 for referral. There are 812+ operational OSCs across India (as of January 2025).

Finding Your Nearest OSC: Contact the Ministry of Women and Child Development or call your state's DLSA (District Legal Services Authority).

3. NGOs and Specialized Support Organizations

National Organizations

Organization	Contact	Services
Aks Foundation	+91 8793 088 814	24/7 crisis helpline for abuse and violence victims. 3000+ calls/year. Community education, workshops
CHILDLINE India	1098 (Toll-free, 24/7)	National emergency service for children in need. 328 cities operational. 1.5+ million calls/ year

All India Women's Conference (AIWC)	Various branches across India	Education, empowerment, women's rights advocacy, support services
Jagori	011-2669 2700, 011-2669 1219	Women's counselling, referral services, legal awareness (Delhi-based, nationwide reach)
Shakti Shalini	011-2437 3737	Crisis intervention, counselling, shelter support (Delhi)
Breakthrough India	011-4166 6101	Gender justice, women empowerment, violence prevention
Azad Foundation	011-49056322	Women's empowerment, economic independence, violence prevention

State-Specific Resources

State	Helpline/ Organization	Contact	Services
Maharashtra	Maharashtra Women's Commission Crisis Helpline	155209	Women's crisis support, legal guidance, referral

Maharashtra	Women Help Line (Mumbai/Thane/ Navi Mumbai)	103 (Toll-free)	Emergency support, crisis intervention
Maharashtra	Women Help Line (Rest of Maharashtra)	1091 (Toll-free)	Emergency support, crisis intervention
Tamil Nadu	Women Helpline 181	181	24/7 support with counselling in Tamil, Telugu, Hindi
Telangana	Domestic Violence Helpline	18002129131	24/7 support in English, Telugu, Hindi
Delhi	Delhi Commission for Women	011-23379181, 011-23370597	Legal protection, counselling, shelter assistance
Delhi	Delhi Women Protection Cell	011-24673366, 011-24674156	Police assistance, legal support
All States	Women Help Desks (WHDs) in Police Stations	Local Police Station	14,658+ WHDs operational across India

4. Legal Resources and Support

Service	Contact/Access	Purpose
District Legal Services Authority (DLSA)	Contact local DLSA	Free legal aid and counselling

Protection Officer under PWDVA	Via OSC or DLSA	Implementation of Protection Orders
Legal Aid Clinics	Via DLSA	Free legal consultation and representation
Mission Shakti Program	Contact State Social Welfare Department	Government scheme for women's safety and empowerment
Beti Bachao Beti Padhao Initiative	Via District Administration	Government program for girls' safety and education

5. **Shelter and Rehabilitation Services**

- Domestic Violence Shelters: Contact your local One-Stop Center or state Social Welfare Department for nearest shelter
- Crisis Centers: Available in major cities; contact 181 for referral
- Rehabilitation Programs: Offered through NGOs and government agencies post-escape from violence

6. **Self-Defence and Safety Training Centers**

- Major Cities: Delhi, Mumbai, Bangalore, Kolkata, Hyderabad, and other metro areas offer self-defence classes
- Contact: Local police women's cells or sports department for information on certified self-defence centers
- Government Support: Some programs are subsidized or free through government women's safety initiatives

7. Mental Health and Counselling

Service	Contact	Availability
AASRA (Suicide Prevention)	9820466726 (Mumbai)	24/7 crisis counselling
iCall	9152987821 or visit icallhelpline.org	Free confidential counselling
National Mental Health Program	Contact State Mental Health Authority	Counselling and psychiatric support

Annexure B: International Helplines and Resources

United States of America

Service	Contact	Availability	Services
National Domestic Violence Hotline	1-800-799-7233 (1-800-799-SAFE)	24/7	Crisis support, safety planning, referral to local resources
Text Support	Text BEGIN to 88788	24/7	Text-based crisis support
TTY (Hearing Impaired)	1-800-787-3224	24/7	Support for deaf/ hard of hearing
National Center for Victims of Crime	1-855-4-VICTIM (1-855-484-2846)	24/7	Victim support and advocacy
StrongHearts Native Helpline	1-844-762-8483	24/7	Support for Native American communities
National LGBT+ Domestic Abuse Hotline	The Network/ La Red: 1-800-832-1901	24/7	Support for LGBTQ+ community
Chat Support	www.thehotline.org (live chat)	24/7	Online chat support

Canada

Service	Contact	Availability	Services
Family Violence Information Line (Alberta)	1-780-310-1818 (Toll-free)	24/7	Crisis support, information, multilingual service
Alberta Abuse Helpline	1-855-443-5722	24/7	Crisis intervention and support
VictimLinkBC (British Columbia)	1-800-563-0808 (Toll-free)	24/7	Crisis support, referral services, multilingual
Domestic Violence Crisis Line (Manitoba)	1-877-977-0007 (Toll-free)	24/7	Emergency support and intervention
Domestic Violence Help Line (Newfoundland & Labrador)	1-888-709-7090	24/7	Crisis support and information
Assaulted Women's Helpline (Ontario)	1-866-863-0511 or text #7233	24/7	Crisis support, multilingual, text option
Fem'aide Support Line (Quebec)	1-877-336-2433	24/7	Crisis support in French
SOS violence conjugale (Quebec)	1-800-363-9010	24/7	Bilingual support for conjugal violence

Hope for Wellness Helpline	1-855-242-3310	24/7	Support for Indigenous peoples
National Helpline	211 (Community and Social Services)	24/7	Referral to local resources

United Kingdom

Service	Contact	Availability	Services
National Domestic Abuse Helpline (England)	0808 2000 247 (Freephone)	24/7	Crisis support, safety planning, trained female advisers
Live Chat	www.nationaldahelpline.org.uk	9am-6pm (Mon-Fri)	Online support, confidential chatbot
BSL Support	Video relay available	10am-6pm (Mon-Fri)	Support via British Sign Language
Domestic and Sexual Abuse Helpline (Northern Ireland)	0808 802 1414 (Freephone)	24/7	Crisis support and information
Online Contact Form	www.nationaldahelpline.org.uk	Anytime	Confidential online reporting

Rape Crisis Helpline (England & Wales)	0808 500 2222	12-2:30pm & 7-9:30pm	Sexual violence support
Women's Aid Directory	www.womensaid.org.uk	Anytime	Find local support services
Respect Phoneline (for abusers)	0808 801 0327 (Mon-Fri, 9am-8pm)	Limited hours	Confidential support for perpetrators
LGBT+ Helpline	0800 999 5428	24/7	Support for LGBTQ+ victims

Australia

Service	Contact	Availability	Services
1800RESPECT	1800 737 732 (Toll-free) or Text 0458 737 732	24/7	National domestic, family and sexual violence counselling
Online Chat & Video Call	www.1800respect.org.au	Mon-Fri 9am-5pm (AEST)	Private online support, no appointment needed
Daisy App	Download free from 1800RESPECT website	Anytime	Privacy-protected resource finder and safety planning

Lifeline	13 11 14 or text 0477 13 11 14 (6pm-midnight)	24/7	Crisis support for personal crisis/ suicide
No to Violence Men's Referral Service	1300 766 491	24/7	Support for men addressing their violent behavior
MensLine Australia	1300 789 978	24/7	Support for men with relationship difficulties
Kids Help Line	1800 55 1800	24/7	Support for children and youth aged 5-25
Elder Abuse Help Line	1300 651 192	24/7	Support for older persons experiencing abuse
State-Specific Services:			
- NSW: Domestic Violence Line	1800 656 463	24/7	State-specific support
- QLD: DV Connect	1800 811 811	24/7	State-specific support
- VIC: Safe Steps	1800 015 188	24/7	State-specific support
- WA: Women's DV Helpline	1800 007 339	24/7	State-specific support
- SA: Crisis Service Line	1800 800 098	24/7	State-specific support

New Zealand

Service	Contact	Availability	Services
Women's Refuge Crisis Line	0800 REFUGE (0800 733 843)	24/7	Immediate crisis support and safe accommodation
Shine (Domestic Abuse Helpline)	0508 744 633 (Toll-free)	9am-11pm daily	Domestic abuse support, webchat available
It's Not OK Info Line	0800 456 450	9am-11pm daily	Information and advice
National Rape & Sexual Abuse Crisis Line	0800 88 33 00	24/7	Sexual violence support, regional connection
Lifeline Aotearoa	0800 543 354 or free text 4357	24/7	Crisis support for depression/suicidal thoughts
Shakti (Ethnic Women)	0800 SHAKTI (0800 742 584)	24/7	Multi-lingual support for Asian and ethnic women
Shama (Sexual Violence - Ethnic Communities)	07 843 3810	24/7	Sexual violence support for ethnic women
Victim Support (Manaaki Tāngata)	0800 842 846	24/7	Free support for crime/trauma victims

Netsafe (Online Harm)	0508 638 723 or text 4282	8am-8pm (weekdays), 9am-5pm (weekends)	Online safety and cyber abuse support
Elder Abuse Response Service	0800 32 668 65 or text 5032	24/7	Support for older persons experiencing abuse
OutLine Aotearoa (Rainbow Support)	0800 688 5463	6-9pm daily	All-ages rainbow community support

Other Key Countries

Country	Service	Contact	Availability
Ireland	Women's Aid National Domestic Violence Helpline	1800 341 900	24/7
South Africa	Childline South Africa	0800 055 555	24/7
South Africa	Gender-Based Violence Command Centre	0800 428 428	24/7
Singapore	National Domestic Violence Hotline	1800 6 DIVORCE (1800 634 8733)	24/7
Malaysia	Women's Aid Organisation Helpline	03-3000 0858	9am-5pm (Mon-Fri)

Philippines	VAWC Hotline	1543 (Nationwide)	24/7
Thailand	Women and Men Network (WMAN)	02-251-6435	Office hours

Annexure C: International Organizations & Online Resources

Global Support Networks

Organization	**Website**	**Services**
United Nations Women	www.unwomen.org	Global advocacy, resources on women's safety
Human Rights Watch	www.hrw.org	Documentation of violence, advocacy
Amnesty International	www.amnesty.org	Human rights advocacy and campaigns
International Justice Mission	www.ijm.org	Combat modern slavery and abuse

Online Chat and Text-Based Support (India)

- iCall: Visit icallhelpline.org for confidential counselling via chat
- Aasra: SMS or call for suicide prevention and crisis support
- NDTV Crisis Alert: Multiple helplines available through their portal

Resources for Creating Safety Plans

- 181 Women Helpline (India): Can guide you through creating a personalized safety plan
- National Domestic Violence Hotline (USA): Free printable safety planning tools at www.thehotline.org
- Women's Aid (UK): Safety planning information at www.womensaid.org.uk

Annexure D: Important Notes and Guidance

Things to Remember:

1. All calls are confidential – These services maintain strict privacy and confidentiality
2. No judgment – Support workers are trained to listen without judging
3. Free services – Most helplines and centers offer free support
4. Multilingual support – Many helplines offer services in multiple languages
5. 24/7 availability – Primary emergency lines are available round-the-clock

When to Call:

- You are experiencing physical, emotional, sexual, or financial abuse
- You are concerned about your safety or someone else's
- You need legal information about protection
- You need counselling or mental health support
- You need information about shelter or safe housing
- You want to create a safety plan

- You are thinking of leaving an abusive situation

What to Do:

- Find a safe, private place to call – Use a friend's phone, a public phone, or call when the abuser is not around
- Be honest about your situation – Support workers need accurate information to help you
- Ask for referrals – Request information about local shelters, legal aid, and counselling services
- Create a safety plan – Develop an escape route, emergency contacts, and important documents location
- Document the abuse – Keep records of incidents, injuries, and threats (in a safe place)
- Reach out to trusted people – Tell friends, family, or neighbors you trust

Important Reminders:

- Your safety comes first – You deserve to live safely
- It's not your fault – Abuse is never the victim's responsibility
- You are not alone – Thousands of people are experiencing similar situations
- Help is available – Professional support can guide you toward safety and healing
- Leave safely – Plan your departure carefully to protect yourself and any children

Annexure E: Resources Specific to Different Situations

If you are a child or adolescent:

- CHILDLINE 1098 (India): 24/7 support for children and young persons
- Kids Help Phone (Canada): 1-800-668-6868
- Kids Help Line (Australia): 1800 55 1800

If you are a man experiencing abuse:

- Aks Foundation (India): +91 8793 088 814
- No to Violence (Australia): 1300 766 491
- MensLine Australia: 1300 789 978
- Respect Phoneline (UK): 0808 801 0327

If you are LGBTQ+:

- The Network/La Red (USA): 1-800-832-1901
- LGBT+ Helpline (UK): 0800 999 5428
- OutLine Aotearoa (New Zealand): 0800 688 5463

If you are from an ethnic/immigrant community:

- Shakti (India/New Zealand): Specific multilingual support
- Shama (New Zealand): Support for ethnic women
- Community organizations in your area

If you are an older person:

- Elder Abuse Response Service (New Zealand): 0800 32 668 65
- Elder Abuse Help Line (Australia): 1300 651 192
- Senior services (contact local authorities)

Last Updated: December 01, 2025

Please note: *While every effort has been made to ensure the accuracy of contact information, phone numbers and services may change. Always verify current information by searching the organization's official website or calling directory assistance if a number is no longer working.*

ABBREVIATIONS

Abbreviation	Full form
AIDS	Acquired Immunodeficiency Syndrome
BBBP	Beti Bachao Beti Padhao
BDSM	Bondage and discipline, dominance and submission, sadism and masochism
CAT	Common Admission Test
CBT	Cognitive Behavioural Therapy
CHD	Coronary heart disease
CMPOs	Child Marriage Prevention Officers
CWC	Child Welfare Committee
DBT	Dialectical Behaviour Therapy
EMDR	Eye Movement Desensitization and Reprocessing
FD	Fixed Deposit
FGM	Female genital mutilation
FMHRIA	Family Homes on Reserves and Matrimonial Interests or Rights Act
GDP	Gross Domestic Product

ICC	Internal Complaints Committee
IIHMR	Indian Institute of Health Management Research
IIM	Indian Institute of Management
IPC	Indian Penal Code
LCC	Local Complaints Committee
MBA	Master of Business Administration
NACO	National AIDS Control Organization
NGO	Non-governmental organisation
NISM	National Institute of Securities Markets
NSC	National Savings Certificate
NPS	National Pension System
OSC	One Stop Centre
PFRDA	Pension Fund Regulatory and Development Authority
PM2.5	Particulate matter 2.5 micrometres or smaller (air pollution)
PPF	Public Provident Fund
PTSD	Post Traumatic Stress Disorder
PWDVA	Protection of Women from Domestic Violence Act, 2005
RD	Recurring Deposit
RM&E	Research, Monitoring and Evaluation
Rs.	Indian rupees
SIP	Systematic Investment Plan
UK	United Kingdom

UNICEF	United Nations Children's Fund
UNODC	United Nations Office on Drugs and Crime
UN Women	United Nations Entity for Gender Equality and the Empowerment of Women
USA	United States of America
VAWA	Violence Against Women Act
WEF	World Economic Forum
WICCI	Women's Indian Chamber of Commerce & Industry

GLOSSARY

Medical

Chloasma: Dark, patchy spots that can appear on the face during pregnancy; sometimes called the "mask of pregnancy".

Coronary heart disease (CHD): A condition where blood flow to the heart is reduced because the arteries supplying the heart become narrowed.

Depression: A mental health condition that can include persistent sadness, loss of interest, low energy, and changes in sleep or appetite.

Estrogen: A key reproductive hormone that rises during pregnancy and influences many body changes.

Fetus: The developing baby in the womb after the early embryonic stage.

Gestational diabetes: High blood sugar first diagnosed during pregnancy; it can make a pregnancy higher-risk and needs medical monitoring.

HIV and AIDS: HIV is a virus that attacks the immune system; AIDS is a later stage of HIV infection when immunity is severely weakened.

Hormones: Chemical messengers produced in the body that help regulate pregnancy, mood, sleep, and many other functions.

Linea nigra: A dark line that may appear from the belly button to the pubic area during pregnancy.

Placenta: An organ that forms during pregnancy and connects the fetus to the uterus, helping exchange oxygen, nutrients, and waste.

PM2.5: Fine air-pollution particles small enough to enter deep into the lungs; high exposure is linked with health risks.

Post Traumatic Stress Disorder (PTSD): A condition that can occur after trauma; symptoms may include nightmares, flashbacks, anxiety, and avoiding reminders.

Preeclampsia: A potentially life-threatening pregnancy complication marked by high blood pressure and signs of organ stress or damage.

Prenatal: The period of pregnancy before childbirth, often used for care and nutrition during pregnancy.

Progesterone: A key pregnancy hormone that supports the uterus and helps maintain pregnancy.

Pulmonary embolism: A serious condition where a blood clot blocks blood flow in the lungs.

Relaxin: A hormone that can loosen ligaments and joints in pregnancy to help prepare the body for childbirth.

Sepsis: A life-threatening reaction to infection that can damage organs.

Trimester: One of three stages of pregnancy: first, second, and third.

Legal

Charge sheet: A formal document filed by police in court stating the charges and evidence after an investigation.

Custody order: A court order about who will care for a child and how custody or access will work.

Domestic violence: Abuse within an intimate or family relationship. It can be physical, sexual, verbal, emotional, or economic.

Dowry death: A death of a woman within a defined period after marriage where evidence shows harassment or cruelty linked to dowry demands.

Emotional abuse: Abuse that harms self-worth or emotional wellbeing, for example constant criticism, humiliation, threats, or manipulation.

Femicide: The killing of women or girls because they are women or girls, often by someone known to them.

Financial abuse: Control or misuse of money to make a partner dependent, for example controlling income, restricting spending, or blocking work.

Gaslighting: A form of manipulation where an abuser makes someone doubt their memory, judgement, or reality.

Gender-based violence: Violence or abuse rooted in unequal power and social norms related to gender.

Indian Penal Code (IPC): India's main criminal law code; certain sections apply to crimes linked to violence against women.

Magistrate: A judicial officer who can hear certain cases and issue orders under laws such as PWDVA.

Monetary order: An order directing the perpetrator to pay financial relief, for example for medical costs or loss of earnings.

Protection order: An order to stop violence, threats, harassment, or contact; it can also restrict entry into certain places.

Protection of Women from Domestic Violence Act, 2005 (PWDVA): An Indian law that provides civil remedies for domestic violence, including protection, residence, monetary, and custody orders.

Residence order: An order that allows a survivor to stay in the shared household or directs the perpetrator to arrange alternative accommodation.

Restraining order: A legal order that restricts a person from contacting, approaching, or harassing someone.

Section 498A: An IPC section addressing cruelty by a husband or his relatives; cruelty can include physical or mental harassment.

Section 304B: An IPC section on dowry death, with legal presumptions when certain conditions are met.

Section 354: An IPC section addressing assault or criminal force intended to outrage a woman's modesty.

One Stop Centre (OSC): A government supported support point where survivors can access multiple services, such as police support, medical help, and counselling.

Internal Complaints Committee (ICC) and Local Complaints Committee (LCC): Bodies created to address workplace sexual harassment complaints, within an organisation (ICC) or at district level (LCC).

Finance

Allowance: Money given in limited amounts by a partner or family member; in abusive situations it can be used to control and restrict.

Fixed Deposit (FD): A bank or post office deposit kept for a fixed period at a fixed interest rate.

Financial insecurity: A situation where meeting basic needs is difficult because income or access to money is unstable or controlled by someone else.

Gross Domestic Product (GDP): A measure of the total value of goods and services produced in a country; used to describe the size of an economy.

National Pension System (NPS): A long-term retirement savings scheme in India regulated by PFRDA.

National Savings Certificate (NSC): A government backed savings product that earns interest over a fixed term.

Pension Fund Regulatory and Development Authority (PFRDA): The Indian regulator that oversees NPS and certain pension products.

Public Provident Fund (PPF): A long-term government backed savings scheme in India with tax benefits, designed for steady savings.

Recurring Deposit (RD): A deposit where you invest a fixed amount every month for a set period and earn interest.

Systematic Investment Plan (SIP): A way to invest a fixed amount at regular intervals, commonly into mutual funds.

Self-growth tools

Affirmations: Short, positive statements repeated regularly to strengthen self-belief and shift internal self-talk.

Agency: The ability to make choices, set goals, and act on them; in this book, it includes rights over one's body, money, and movement.

Forgiveness: A personal process of letting go of the hold of past harm. It does not mean excusing abuse or giving an abuser another chance.

Graphology and graphotherapy: Graphology is the analysis of handwriting; graphotherapy uses handwriting changes as a self-development tool.

Gratitude internalization meditation: A practice of focusing attention on gratitude, allowing the feeling to settle in the body and mind.

Ho'oponopono: A Hawaiian practice used as a self-reflection and release tool, often involving phrases like "I'm sorry, please forgive me, thank you, I love you".

Kinesthesia: The sense of the body from within. The book uses this to describe connecting to bodily feelings and signals.

Mirror exercise: A self-work practice of looking into a mirror and speaking to yourself with kindness, reassurance, or encouragement.

Trigger alert: A short warning that the next section contains potentially distressing content, so readers can choose how to engage.

Visualization: A mental practice of imagining a desired safe future or outcome in detail, to strengthen confidence and motivation.